"Bateson has an extremely interesting mind and the ability to express herself with extraordinary literary felicity. . . . Too much truth steams behind the quiet elegance of these passages."
—*The New York Times Book Review*

"I want to hail Bateson for finding—creating, really—a literary form that reflects the way women commonly reason and talk. . . . Bateson makes an addition to women's literary culture that feels absolutely true. . . . In the end we are left reflecting in amazement on the marvelous delicacy and scope of a whole woven discourse about a community of friends and the larger human community in which they thrive. . . . A fascinating book."—*The Boston Globe*

"Mary Catherine Bateson has written about women but not just for women. Everyone can gain from this book, me especially."
—Bill Moyers

"It is among the most inspiring books about contemporary living. It is potentially helpful to women, and men as well, as they make decisions for themselves and those close to them."
—*Sunday Boston Herald*

"The book proposes an exciting idea: that marginality can be celebrated for its space and creativity, that women may be on their way to establishing a new social ecology. . . . Bateson is passionate, convincing, and well informed. . . . I admire her attempt to turn the discontinuity that women so often encounter toward a feminine ideal of interdependence, nurturing, and imagination."—*7 Days*

COMPOSING
A
LIFE

COMPOSING
A
LIFE

Mary Catherine Bateson

GROVE PRESS
New York

Excerpt from "Portrait by a Neighbour" by Edna St. Vincent Millay. From *Collected Poems,* Harper & Row. Copyright © 1922, 1950 by Edna St. Vincent Millay. Reprinted by permission.

"spring is like a perhaps hand" by e. e. cummings. Copyright 1925, © 1973, 1976 by Trustees for the e. e. cummings Trust.

Published simultaneously in Canada
Printed in the United States of America

Library of Congress Cataloging-in-Publication Data

Bateson, Mary Catherine.
    Composing a life / by Mary Catherine Bateson.
    ISBN-13: 978-0-8021-3804-0
    1. Life. I. Title.

BD431.B32   1989   302.5—dc20   89-6553

Design by Tim O'Keeffe

Grove Press
an imprint of Grove/Atlantic, Inc.
841 Broadway
New York, NY 10003

Distributed by Publishers Group West

www.groveatlantic.com

09 10 11 12 13   10 9 8 7 6 5

This one is for Vanni.

ACKNOWLEDGMENTS

THIS BOOK is rooted in friendship. Whenever I open it, I will be reminded of what I owe to the four women whose lives, with my own, are mingled here. Ellen Bassuk, Johnnetta Cole, Alice d'Entremont, and Joan Erikson provided not only material for a book but also wisdom for my own life. I have tried to use the memories they entrusted to me in ways that would not damage their unfolding stories and the lives of others they care about. None of them has reviewed this material, so I must hope for their forgiveness for any error or infelicity, and I thank them for their trust and for the hours we spent together.

Some of the narratives recounted here are painful or critical. They are based on individual points of view, so there are surely other points of view not represented. Thus, I find myself thanking those I did not interview, many of whom would have cooperated willingly, and apologizing to them for the choice of a narrow focus for this research. Beyond that, I want to acknowledge especially the individuals not mentioned here who helped me during crucial periods of my life. Portions of this book speak of Amherst College, and for all my criticisms, I want to emphasize the wealth of friendships and the decency and quality of mind I found in many there.

I made a decision early on to organize my writing around the stories of women whose lives were productive and successful, but I learned as much from women I have known whose lives have been tragic. I want to take this opportunity to thank them for what they have taught me and to express the hope that through this work their experiences too will benefit others. I also want to thank all the other men and women who have talked to me about their lives, contributing to this process, and to wish them well.

The narratives about individuals provide a framework for musings about the shape of individual lives, about relationships and commitments, and about gender. Extensive scholarly apparatus would be inappropriate for this format, but I want to note here that I have learned from many academic conversations and from the increasing analytic literature on these subjects. Joan and Erik Erikson especially have contributed to the intellectual framework of this book. Other key ideas echo the work of my parents, Margaret Mead and Gregory Bateson, for whom themes of cooperation and competition, symmetry and complementarity recurred repeatedly.

I am especially grateful to my husband, J. Barkev Kassarjian, and my daughter, Sevanne Kassarjian, known as Vanni, whose key roles in my life are reflected in this book. Both were essential to its writing. Barkev and I have been married for nearly thirty years; the hours spent reviewing drafts and discussing these ideas have evolved into an intimate collaboration that deserves far more than the pro forma acknowledgments often given to spouses. Vanni represents the future I wish to understand.

I have had the benefit of careful readings and commentary on the manuscript from Barkev and Vanni, from my friends Barbara Kreiger and Alan Lelchuk, and from my editor Ann Godoff. I would also like to thank my agent, John Brockman, and the John Simon Guggenheim Memorial Foundation for a fellowship in 1987–88 that supported this project.

CONTENTS

EMERGENT
VISIONS

THIS IS A STUDY of five artists engaged in that act of creation that engages us all—the composition of our lives. Each of us has worked by improvisation, discovering the shape of our creation along the way, rather than pursuing a vision already defined.

In a stable society, composing a life is somewhat like throwing a pot or building a house in a traditional form: the materials are known, the hands move skillfully in tasks familiar from thousands of performances, the fit of the completed whole in the common life is understood. Traditional styles of pottery or building are not usually rigid; they respond to chance and allow a certain scope for individual talent and innovation. But the traditional craftsperson does not face the task of solving every problem for the first time. In a society like our own, we make a sharp contrast between creativity and standardization, yet even those who work on factory production lines must craft their own lives, whether graceful and assured or stunted and askew.

Today, the materials and skills from which a life is composed are no longer clear. It is no longer possible to follow the paths of previous generations. This is true for both men and women, but it is especially true for women, whose whole lives no longer need be dominated by the rhythms of procreation and the dependencies that these created, but who still must live with the discontinuities of female biology and still must balance conflicting demands. Our lives not only take new directions; they are subject to repeated redirection, partly because of the extension of our years of health and productivity. Just as the design of a building or of a vase must be rethought when the scale is changed, so must the design of lives. Many of the most basic concepts we use to construct a sense of self or the design of a life have changed their meanings: Work. Home. Love. Commitment.

For many years I have been interested in the arts of improvisation, which involve recombining partly familiar materials in new ways, often in ways especially sensitive to context, interaction, and response. When I was a teenager, I used to go to the house of my mother's sister Liza and hear her son, the jazz flutist Jeremy Steig, playing and practicing with his friends, jamming in the back room, varying and revarying familiar phrases. "Practicing improvisation" was clearly not a contradiction. Jazz exemplifies artistic activity that is at once individual and communal, performance that is both repetitive and innovative, each participant sometimes providing background support and sometimes flying free.

The concept of improvisation stayed in the back of my mind later, as I became interested in studying languages and in thinking about the ways in which each speaker learns to combine and vary familiar components to say something new to fit a particular context and evoke a particular response, sometimes something of very great beauty or significance, but always improvisational and always adaptive. In college, I became fascinated by Arabic poetry, particularly the early poems from the oral tradition in which poets combined memorization and improvisation to fit particular situations. Creativity of this kind has now been well studied. It can be discerned in the Homeric epics, which show every sign of having been produced in this way; and equally well in the rhetorical style of a Martin Luther King, Jr., with its echoes of the rousing preaching in the black churches.

This is a book about life as an improvisatory art, about the ways we combine familiar and unfamiliar components in response to new situations, following an underlying grammar and an evolving aesthetic. It started from a disgruntled reflection on my own life as a sort of desperate improvisation in which I was constantly trying to make something coherent from conflicting elements to fit rapidly changing settings. At times, I pictured myself frantically rummaging through the refrigerator and the kitchen cabinets, convinced that somewhere I would find the odds and ends that could be combined at the last minute to make a meal for unexpected guests, hoping to be rescued by serendipity. A good meal, like a poem or a life, has a certain balance and diversity, a certain coherence and fit. As one learns to cope in the kitchen, one no longer duplicates whole meals but rather manipulates components and the way they are put together. The improvised meal will be different from the planned meal, and certainly riskier, but rich with the possibility of delicious surprise. Improvisation can be either a last resort or an established way of evoking creativity. Sometimes a pattern chosen by default can become a path of preference.

This book attempts to turn my question around, to look at problems in terms of the creative opportunities they present. I believe that our aesthetic sense, whether in works of art or in lives, has overfocused on the stubborn struggle toward a single goal rather than on the fluid, the protean, the improvisatory. We see achievement as purposeful and monolithic, like the sculpting of a massive tree trunk that has first to be brought from the forest and then shaped by long labor to assert the artist's vision, rather than something crafted from odds and ends, like a patchwork quilt, and lovingly used to warm different nights and bodies. Composing a life has a metaphorical relation to many different arts, including architecture and dance and cooking. In the visual arts, a variety of disparate elements may be arranged to form a simultaneous whole, just as we combine our simultaneous commitments. In the temporal arts, like music, a sequential diversity may be brought into harmony over time. In still other arts, such as homemaking or gardening, choreography or administration, complexity is woven in both space and time.

When the choices and rhythms of lives change, as they have in our time, the study of lives becomes an increasing preoccupation. This is especially true now for women. The biography sections of bookstores continue to expand as scholars chronicle the few famous women and discover others whose achievements have not yet been noted and honored. Others try to understand the texture of the hidden and unrecorded lives of women in our own and other cultures. The women's history movement has many different elements, some of them parallel to the black history movement: the need to make the invisible visible, the desire to provide role models and empower aspirations, the possibility that by setting a number of life histories side by side, we will be enabled to recognize common patterns of creativity that have not been acknowledged or fostered. The process starts with the insistence that there have been great achievements by women and people of color. Inevitably, it moves on to a rethinking of the concept of achievement.

Women today read and write biographies to gain perspective on their own lives. Each reading provokes a dialogue of comparison and recognition, a process of memory and articulation that makes one's own experience available as a lens of empathy. We gain even more from comparing notes and trying to understand the choices of our friends. When one has matured surrounded by implicit disparagement, the undiscovered self is an unexpected resource. Self-knowledge is empowering.

Nevertheless, there is a pattern deeply rooted in myth and folklore that recurs in biography and may create inappropriate expectations and blur our ability to see the actual shape of lives. Much biography of exceptional people is built around the image of a quest, a journey through a timeless

5

landscape toward an end that is specific, even though it is not fully known. The pursuit of a quest is a pilgrim's progress in which it is essential to resist the transitory contentment of attractive way stations and side roads, in which obstacles are overcome because the goal is visible on the horizon, onward and upward. The end is already apparent in the beginning. The model of an ordinary successful life that is held up for young people is one of early decision and commitment, often to an educational preparation that launches a single rising trajectory. Ambition, we imply, should be focused, and young people worry about whether they are defining their goals and making the right decisions early enough to get on track. You go to medical school and this determines later alternatives, whether you choose prosperity in the suburbs or the more dramatic and exceptional life of discovery and dedication. Graduation is supposed to be followed by the first real job, representing a step on an ascending ladder. We don't expect long answers when we ask children what they want to be when they grow up, any more than we expect a list of names in response to questions about marriage. In fact, assumptions about careers are not unlike those about marriage; the real success stories are supposed to be permanent and monogamous.

These assumptions have not been valid for many of history's most creative people, and they are increasingly inappropriate today. The landscape through which we move is in constant flux. Children cannot even know the names of the jobs and careers that will be open to them; they must build their fantasies around temporary surrogates. Goals too clearly defined can become blinkers. Just as it is less and less possible to replicate the career of a parent, so it will become less and less possible to go on doing the same thing through a lifetime. In the same way, we will have to change our sense of the transitory and learn to see success in marriages that flourish for a time and then end. Increasingly, we will recognize the value in lifetimes of continual redefinition, following the Biblical injunction, "Whatsoever thy hand findeth to do, do it with thy might" (Ecclesiastes 9:10).

Many of society's casualties are men and women who assumed they had chosen a path in life and found that it disappeared in the underbrush. These are easiest to recognize in areas where continuity used to be greatest.

In the American Midwest, farmers have been losing their farms and finding themselves without path or purpose. Working on land that often has been in the family for several generations, they have interpreted their lives in terms of continuity even as the economics and the technological nature of farming have been steadily changing. The story of the foreclosed farmer is comparable to that of the displaced homemaker who assumed that marriage defined both her work and her security. She has been no more an idle dependent than the farmer, but she too defined herself in terms of a niche that proved evanescent.

Others do not become visible casualties, because they are protected by contracts or union rules from facing the challenges of change. What they lose, and what the society loses through them, is the possibility of learning and development.

In the academic world, the tenure system still supplies a high degree of security and campuses still project serene images of continuity. Young teachers who choose or are forced to leave often feel that their lives are ending, like foreclosed farmers and displaced homemakers. But watching men and women who have left as they reconstruct and redirect their lives, I have become convinced that for many of them this discontinuity has been a move from stagnation to new challenge and growth, just as divorce often represents progress rather than failure.

All too often, men and women are like battered wives or abused children. We hold on to the continuity we have, however profoundly it is flawed. If change were less frightening, if the risks did not seem so great, far more could be lived. One of the striking facts of most lives is the recurrence of threads of continuity, the re-echoing of earlier themes, even across deep rifts of change, but when you watch people damaged by their dependence on continuity, you wonder about the nature of commitment, about the need for a new and more fluid way to imagine the future.

The twentieth century has been called the century of the refugee because of the vast numbers of people uprooted by war and politics from their homes and accustomed lives. At the time of the Iranian revolution, my husband and I had lived in Iran for seven years. We had to adjust to the loss of our property there, including our books and papers, the loss of jobs, and the destruction of the institutions we had devoted those years to building. But seven years is minor compared to the dislocations that others faced. Some adjusted quickly, finding ways to affirm themselves and their skills in a new environment, bridging discontinuity. Others are still adrift, burdened by the broken assumptions of continuity.

Another set of discontinuities is created by the shifting business and industrial environment. Towns that have depended on a single industry for generations suddenly find half their people unemployed, with no way to learn new skills or find new homes. In this era of hostile takeovers and leveraged buyouts, continuity at the executive level is suddenly interrupted, businesses are restructured, and career managers find themselves facing "outplacement." Even monks and nuns must learn new skills as neighborhoods change around their monasteries; religious orders today must plan on turnover and constantly revised vocations. The fine old idea of a path and a commitment turns out to be illusory for many people, not only for geographical and political refugees but for cultural refugees displaced by the discontinuities of custom and economy. Even those who continue to wear the same professional label survive only because they have altered what they do. Being effective as a banker or a restaurateur or a general means that one has relearned one's craft more than once.

It is time now to explore the creative potential of interrupted and conflicted lives, where energies are not narrowly focused or permanently pointed toward a single ambition. These are not lives without commitment, but rather lives in which commitments are continually refocused and redefined. We must invest time and passion in specific goals and yet at the same time acknowledge that these are mutable. The circumstances of women's lives now and in the past provide examples for new ways of thinking about the lives of both men and women. What are the possible transfers of learning when life is a collage of different tasks? How does creativity flourish on distraction? What insights arise from the experience of multiplicity and ambiguity? And at what point does desperate improvisation become significant achievement? These are important questions in a world in which we are all increasingly strangers and sojourners. The knight errant, who finds his challenges along the way, may be a better model for our times than the knight who is questing for the Grail.

Current research on women often focuses on a single aspect or stage of life. Dissection is an essential part of scientific method, and it is particularly tempting to disassemble a life composed of odds and ends, to describe the pieces separately. Unfortunately, when this is done the pattern and loving labor in the patchwork is lost. This book started from the effort to explore different ways of thinking about my own life, to see its pattern as a whole, and to illuminate it by looking at the lives of other women I admire, lives of achievement as well as caring, that have a unitary quality in spite of being improvisations.

The person who first came to mind in thinking about this project was Joan Erikson. I have known Joan and her husband Erik Erikson, friends of my parents, since my childhood. Whatever composing a life is all about, Joan seemed to me to be someone who, at least for her time, got it right. She has three grown-up children and a career that includes several books of her own as well as a complex weave of collaboration with her husband's work, which led Brown University in 1972 to give them simultaneous honorary degrees. Joan was trained as a dancer and dance educator, the first of several careers that became subordinated to childbearing and a husband's work. Now in her eighties, she still moves like a dancer, conveying to younger women the sense of beauty transcending age, and she and Erik hold hands in the street. Joan's creative work has been done in scraps of rescued space and time, in marginal roles that have had to be invented again and again. The theme of improvisation is very clear. Once she described to me how she got started in jewelry making:

"I used to find places in the house to work, a hole here or a hole there, and after I'd gotten far enough along so I could do something, I asked a man who was a very good craftsman in Berkeley to let me work in his workshop and he promptly said, 'No way!' " Joan laughed. "So I said, 'Well, just wait a minute, I'll tell you what I want, I want to learn a few skills from you. I'm not good enough to be your apprentice, but there are a few things you could teach me on maybe a Saturday morning to keep me going.' And he said, 'I don't even know if you have any skill or imagination or anything else.' I didn't have much to show him, just a few things I had made, but I guess I was kind of persistent, so he gave me a box of junk—you know, when you're working you always have some bits and pieces here or there—and he said, 'Put me something together out of that.' And when I did he said, 'Humph, so when can you come?' It was very sweet. My gosh, craftsmen are so nice. When they're nice they're very generous. I went on doing that for quite a while, coming in with a list of things I needed to know. But the next year he left to teach, and when he left he gave me his workbench and the tools he didn't want to take with him. At that point I had to find a better workshop, so I added something onto the garage for a little place to work." Several years later, Joan's designs were appearing in regional and national exhibits.

On the whole, women today follow their interests into more formal careers, but there remain unexpected similarities between the multiple commitments and discontinuities they face and the patterns of Joan's improvisations. Because I have always earned an income and had a professional title, as an instructor or a professor or a dean, the course of my life that led to the writing of this book looked in many ways very different from Joan's. I rushed my degrees to fit in with my marriage instead of abandoning them, and I have taught or done research in linguistics and anthropology ever since. But the underlying assumptions of my life have until recently been very much the same as Joan's: that family life would be constructed around my husband's decisions about his career—which led him first to the Philippines and then to Iran—and my career would be subordinated to or contingent on the needs of family life, a husband, and a daughter. These assumptions were standard when I grew up, and we are not yet free of them. They continue to order many two-career families.

In my own case, they represented a certain rebellion as well as a coming to terms with cultural norms. My mother, Margaret Mead, was one of the outstanding women of her time, probably the best known of American anthropologists. She constructed her life around professional constancies and made her marriages fit. She left two husbands and was then herself rejected by the third, my father, the anthropologist Gregory Bateson. I had a rich and unusual childhood, with many adult caretakers, and I made my own synthesis from the models offered by my parents and the others I saw around me, assuming I would have a professional life of my own, but that I would construct it around my husband's career. Today I can see that even in our differences my mother and I shared the struggle to combine multiple commitments, always liable to conflict or interruption. Each of us had to search in ambiguity for her own kind of integrity, learning to adapt and improvise in a culture in which we could only partly be at home.

Fluidity and discontinuity are central to the reality in which we live. Women have always lived discontinuous and contingent lives, but men today are newly vulnerable, which turns women's traditional adaptations into a resource. Historically, even women who devoted themselves to homemaking and childcare have had to put together a mosaic of activities and resolve conflicting demands on their time and attention. The physical rhythms of reproduction and maturation create sharper discontinuities in women's lives than in men's, the shifts of puberty and menopause, of pregnancy, birth, and lactation, the mirroring adaptations to the unfolding lives of children, their departures and returns, the ebb and flow of dependency, the birth of grandchildren, the probability of widowhood. As a result, the ability to shift from one preoccupation to another, to divide one's attention, to improvise in new circumstances, has always been important to women. In the Philippines, when my training in Arabic linguistics was unusable, I retooled as a cultural anthropologist, but this is a less demanding shift than the shift from wife to mother, although perhaps a lonelier one. By examining the way women have coped with discontinuities in their lives, we may discover important clues that will help us all, men and women, cope with our unfolding lives.

Because of the conditions of my life, I have had to learn something many of my academic colleagues don't seem to know: that continuity is the exception in twentieth-century America, and that adjusting to discontinuity is not an idiosyncratic problem of my own but the emerging problem of our era. "How," a young assistant professor wailed to me once, when I was Dean of the Faculty at Amherst College, "can they expect to know me well enough to make a judgment in only three years?" Because of our periods overseas, I had never held a job for over three years, other than that of wife and mother, and plenty of couples decide within less than three years that they know each other all too well.

In many ways, constancy is an illusion. After all, our ancestors were immigrants, many of them moving on every few years; today we are migrants in time. Unless teachers can hold up a model of lifelong learning and adaptation, graduates are likely to find themselves trapped into obsolescence as the world changes around them. Of any stopping place in life, it is good to ask whether it will be a good place from which to go on as well as a good place to remain.

I was in my mid-forties when I left Amherst. We are preoccupied today with midlife crises because these moments of reassessment and redirection occur now with half a lifetime of productivity still ahead, when opportunity still beckons beyond perplexity. We must expect that, over time, such moments will occur repeatedly, that we will live many lives. I found myself looking again at a patchwork of achievements both personal and professional and questioning how they fit together: whether they composed—or began to compose—a life; whether indeed the model of improvisation might prove more creative and appropriate to the twentieth century than the model of single-track ambition. Thinking about myself and about other women I have known, some of them proud and contented and others embittered and angry, I decided that the place to look for the key to new patterns was in lives that were clearly composite. Such a key may be helpful in understanding not only how women make sense of interrupted and discontinuous lives, but also in understanding the goals of education and the terms of men's lives today. All of us are increasingly torn between conflicting loyalties, yet our lives are longer and more full of possibilities than ever before.

Change proposes constancy: What is the ongoing entity of which we can say that it has assumed a new form? A composite life poses the recurring riddle of what the parts have in common. Why is a raven like a writing desk? How is a lady like a soldier? Why is caring for an infant like designing a computer program? How is the study of ancient poetry like the design of universities? If your opinions and commitments appear to change from year to year or decade to decade, what are the more abstract underlying convictions that have held steady, that might never have become visible without the surface variation?

I have chosen to explore these subjects by examining five lives—my own and those of four friends. All have faced discontinuities and divided energies, yet each has been rich in professional achievement and in personal relationships—in love and work. We are different from each other, but we have many things in common. This book is the outcome of a process of conversation and reflection. It is a way of making these lives available to others in a form that differs both from the extended narratives of heroic biography or case history on the one hand and the lost individuality of the survey on the other.

These are not representative lives. They do not constitute a statistical sample—only, I hope, an interesting one. As I have worked over the material, I have become aware that the portions of these life histories that interest me most are the echoes from one life to another, the recurrent common themes. Teasing these out of a wealth of material and conversation and recognizing aspects of my own experience in different forms has been the process that I found personally most freeing and illuminating. We need to look at multiple lives to test and shape our own. Growing up with two talented and very different parents, I have never looked for single role models. I believe in the need for multiple models, so that it is possible to weave something new from many different threads.

The recognition that many people lead lives of creative makeshift and improvisation surely has implications for how the next generation is educated and what we tell our sons and daughters. The American version of liberal-arts education, since it is not closely career oriented, provides a good base for lifelong learning and for retraining when that becomes necessary, but the institutions themselves often exemplify the opposite. Grassy campuses across the country beckon graciously to children leaving home for the first time; although they are no more than way stations for their graduates, they still suggest the old norm of lifetime commitment and security. For those who work in them, they represent it even more clearly than a monastery would, or a family farm. In effect, the best of our young men and women are educated by faculties deeply committed to continuity. Most of them have spent their entire lives in a single institution, often surrounded by the apparent tranquility of a small town, and may no longer be intellectually flexible or open to change. Ancient walls covered with ivy are more lovely than tents and trailers, but we need to teach the skills for coming into a new place and quickly making it into a home. When we speak to our children about our own lives, we tend to reshape our pasts to give them an illusory look of purpose. But our children are unlikely to be able to define their goals and then live happily ever after. Instead, they will need to reinvent themselves again and again in response to a changing environment.

Once you begin to see these lives of multiple commitments and multiple beginnings as an emerging pattern rather than an aberration, it takes no more than a second look to discover the models for that reinvention on every side, to look for the followers of visions that are not fixed but that evolve from day to day. Each such model, like each individual work of art, is a comment about the world outside the frame. Just as change stimulates us to look for more abstract constancies, so the individual effort to compose a life, framed by birth and death and carefully pieced together from disparate elements, becomes a statement on the unity of living. These works of art, still incomplete, are parables in process, the living metaphors with which we describe the world.

IN THE COMPANY
OF FRIENDS

ALTHOUGH I HAVE NEVER SEEN HER DANCE, I have always thought of Joan as a dancer, whatever work she was doing, tall and graceful and athletic, with practical strong hands. She wears clothes that are fluid and uncluttered, flaring skirts and turtleneck sweaters and handwoven shawls. She often wears gray or black, which provides a background for jewelry of her own design and making. Often, her jewelry combines interesting beads from all over the world, the human concerns of prayer and exchange and mnemonic expressed in the fashioning of material counters. Joan explored the range of meaning of beads in her book, *The Universal Bead,* so every necklace or pair of earrings that she makes is shaped by scholarship as well as artistry. She has represented to me a distinctive relationship with the physical and material world, one in which the careful handling of metal or ceramic or wool becomes an expression of more abstract issues of human caring and strength.

Women's lives have always been grounded in the physical by the rhythms of their bodies and the giving and receiving of concrete and specific tokens of love, a ring or a teaspoon of cough syrup. Whenever this project has led me into academic abstractions about roles and institutions, I have used my images of Joan to keep me rooted in the loving experience of the sensory and the material. Joan is the oldest of the women who worked with me on this project. She seems to know fully who she is and how the pieces of her life fit together. She has combined her youthful identity as a dancer with her later work as a craftsperson and writer into a single unity, just as each of us, in our different landscapes, composes a life out of the materials that come to hand.

Ellen Bassuk, a physician and psychiatrist, is the youngest in the group and my most recent acquaintance. I met her in 1983 at Radcliffe's Bunting Institute, a women's center for advanced studies, during a period of transition in both our lives, when I was working on a memoir of my parents. I became fascinated by Ellen's work when she gave the colloquium that each Bunting fellow gives, speaking of the men and women she had interviewed and tested in Boston's shelters for the homeless. Standing by the podium, with the disheveled images of loneliness and despair projected on a screen behind her, she was concerned and professional, and yet she projected an undercurrent of passion.

In those days, homelessness was just beginning to be a matter of national concern, and the issue was new to me. Ellen had become aware of it early, publishing her first related research in 1976. She had tracked the slow increase in chronically ill and isolated patients in the emergency room at Boston's Beth Israel Hospital, where she directed the emergency psychiatric service. Because she recognized the echo of an earlier period when she was assigned as a psychiatric resident to a state mental hospital, she was one of the first to draw the connection between the deinstitutionalization of the mentally ill that occurred in the seventies and the rise in homelessness.

"Emergency services are the court of last resort," she explained to me. "They cater to people who are not in the system and don't have insurance, who want to remain anonymous and don't want to deal with fixed hours or appointments. Compared to the rest of the population in the hospital, they are poorer and sicker, with a lot fewer psychosocial supports. The emergency room is the first place that reflects changes in social policy that uproot people, so when deinstitutionalization occurred, the ER was the first place that began to see the chronics in any numbers."

Ellen's career has involved accepting undesirable assignments and then discovering the intellectual and human challenge of attending those who have not merited attention. "There are certain jobs in big-time teaching hospitals that are almost reserved for women, because in the psychiatric hierarchy they are seen as less desirable than running the inpatient or outpatient units where the psychotherapy goes on. Crisis intervention is not valued in the same way as psychotherapy. In our department, the people who had these jobs were usually women, and women never had those other jobs, the core jobs. The ER is the most dangerous and most service-oriented department in psychiatry. It's open twenty-four hours a day, and if someone comes in you're up, you've got to move fast. It's action oriented and it's really dangerous down there because anybody can walk in and get out of control, an acute unmedicated psychotic or someone on PCP who might have a weapon." Ironically, the risks make such unpopular assignments harder for a woman to decline than for a man; a woman who declines may be suspected of weakness, while a man is credited with ambition.

I found it easier to visualize Ellen meeting with private patients in the upstairs consulting room in her house, where we taped our sessions, than in the hectic environment of the emergency room. She does not evoke images of crisis, but instead projects the concern and good sense that may be exactly what is needed to defuse a volatile situation. She has the coloring of a redhead, with translucent fair skin, a few freckles, and green eyes, but her short curly hair is more nearly auburn.

Ellen's work involves listening, and she listens well, conveying an impression of neutrality and thoughtful integration leavened with warmth and flashes of mischief. Her presentation at the Bunting colloquium was medical and objective, peppered with statistics, moving into advocacy as we discussed it afterwards and she set out to draw on my background in anthropological fieldwork to supplement her own research training. Later I learned that even as she spoke, she was shifting her focus from homeless individuals to homeless mothers and children and restructuring her professional life to gain the flexibility to have children herself while sustaining her research. By the time we began work on this book, Ellen had a son, Danny, and she and her husband were working their way through the harrowing process of adopting a second child.

Alice d'Entremont is an electrical engineer whose experience has ranged from the design of experimental research equipment for Skylab to being the chief executive officer of a new high-tech company struggling to establish a commercial niche. Much of her work is beyond my understanding, and yet her aesthetic pleasure in what she does, her sense that technology is the art form of the twentieth century, provides us with a bridge of intelligibility. She lives surrounded by plants that flourish and proliferate until she passes them on to friends with less nurturing hands.

I met Alice in 1979 after she and Jack, a creative inventor and entrepreneur whom my husband and I had known since the sixties, became lovers and then colleagues. Together they struggled with elusive questions of electronics and financing until Jack's death in 1985, spending their free time cooking together and searching out the finest ingredients in Boston's Italian markets. When I asked Alice to work on this project, she came and stayed for a week with me in New Hampshire in the summer of 1987. She walked in the woods and together we taped long interviews about her life.

It was the first vacation she had had after a long, turbulent time, and she used our interviews to sort through the dramas of the last two years and their earlier roots. She struggled to explain to me the technical issues in her work with computer imaging and then commandeered my kitchen to make squash-flower fritters and ratatouille and persuaded me that the time had come to paint the new kitchen cabinets.

Alice is a woman of vivid contrasts, combining delicacy with drama and sexiness. She loves chunky silver jewelry and wears large modernistic earrings and brooches, like a habit of diffidence overcome. She is slim but broad shouldered, with the kind of nose that is said to impart character. Her short hair has turned to silver, but her eyebrows remain dark.

Alice defies stereotypes. Back in the days of Skylab, when there were very few women engineers indeed, Alice showed up to tell a conference of senior NASA officials that their equipment would have to be altered in very basic and very expensive ways, wearing a miniskirt and purple tights, relying on her professional competence to establish her right to speak. When she became an executive and a senior engineer, she made a few sartorial concessions, occasionally even wearing what the advertisers call power suits, but she is too quick and vehement to look convincingly managerial.

Alice's descriptions of her childhood in Rumania were filled with reflections on nonconformity and reminiscences of escaping through the window and over the roof to play with neighborhood children and dogs. "I was always told not to go to the gypsies, because they had all sorts of diseases and they stole children, but of course that made me go. And I would indeed pick up worms or lice, and my granma would say, 'You must have been with the gypsies,' and I would say, 'Me?' And we would cure all these things, and I would go back. They did outrageous things—the children didn't wear underpants, and we would take our shoes off and walk in the fields in the fresh cowshit, and the granma didn't really scold. I developed the idea very early that if there were rules that didn't make sense, you had to think carefully about how you broke them. If you got caught, well, OK, you got caught, but that was not a reason to stop thinking."

Shortly after we began work on this project, Johnnetta Cole, once my neighbor in Amherst, Massachusetts, was selected to be the first black woman president of Spelman College in Atlanta, Georgia. Not one but two of her friends celebrated the occasion by sending her pairs of white gloves, spoofing the gentility she would need to adopt, but also underlining the particularity needed in designing a new role. Johnnetta's beauty is distinctively Afro-American; she has long bones and a finely molded skull. When we spoke of her conflict with her mother back in the sixties about leaving her hair unstraightened in a compact "natural," she said to me (as one anthropologist to another) that she likes the "dolichocephalic look." Her honey-colored skin and blue-green eyes refer back to a white grandfather, a German immigrant, but they also evoke the invidious comparisons of shade that have inhibited emerging clarity about black ways of beauty.

It is not easy, putting on a new identity as a college president, to learn to express the new role without meeting a stranger in the mirror. Every day, said Johnnetta, who was once a campus radical in a black motorcycle jacket, she includes at least one detail in her clothing that defies conformity—a carved ivory Janus-faced pendant, made as the emblem of a Liberian secret society; a cowrie-studded belt; or fabric hand-woven by a friend. All the issues of identity and presentation of self are complicated by the need to provide intelligible role models, for college presidents are supposed to project not only policies but lifestyles.

A week after Johnnetta moved to Atlanta in 1987, I arrived for a ten-day stay in Reynolds Cottage, the presidential residence that sits in the middle of the shady and gracious Spelman campus, which was tranquil and empty in the middle of summer. She showed me around what is really a mansion, her comments moving between the mementos of Spelman's past and her plans for her own tenancy. Then we took our drinks out onto a screened verandah as a storm burst and we were surrounded by sudden darkness and pouring rain, providing a curious privacy in this most public space. We were both thrown back into memories of tropical cloudbursts and started talking about Johnnetta's time as a researcher in Liberia and the Caribbean and mine in the Philippines. When the rain stopped, the smells were completely different from our memories: lawns, the trees of temperate climates, and the flowers of the South.

Johnnetta pointed out an area along the outside of the terrace, planted with the flower called impatiens, compliments of "The Cosby Show," which had taped a program two months earlier at the Spelman campus, set up as the fictional Hillman College. I wondered whether someone on the show chose that flower deliberately to refer to the long slow pace of progress in opportunity: the centuries before higher education became accessible to women until the first

tentative beginnings in the 1830s, the years before the Civil
War when it was illegal in Georgia to teach slaves to read,
and the extra decades it has taken before the opportunities
converged. Finally, it has become possible to give leadership
in the education of young Afro-American women into the
hands of a black woman, both at fictional Hillman and at real
life Spelman. Impatience. Impatience and gracious living.
When Johnnetta was formally inaugurated as president, Bill
and Camille Cosby announced a donation to the college of
twenty million dollars.

As Johnnetta and I sat on that verandah that first night
in Atlanta, our talk was shaped by the fact that we are both
anthropologists and we have both been involved in educational administration, simultaneously inventing ourselves,
offering models, and trying to understand the process of
change and the range of human possibility. We had met for
the first time a decade and a half before, at a conference on
anthropology and "relevance," the word of the day. I had
barely gotten to know Johnnetta in that group; instead of
socializing with the other participants, I had raced off during
the breaks to the hotel where my godmother was looking
after my infant daughter, Vanni. My memories are a mix of
the problems of baby food and diapers and the shock of the
United States' bombing of Cambodia and the shootings at
Kent State that occurred even as we tried to formulate a
statement of the contribution that anthropology could make.

Each of these women spoke of other men and women, so that
each story became a lens for looking at other lives—the

teachers and parents who shaped and supported us, the careers of husbands and lovers, the development of children and students, the slow healing of patients, the shared excitement of collaboration. We are all aware of living in a time when women are exploring new territory; we are all aware that these explorations will affect our understandings of men's lives as well, and of the human condition. We have followed different roads with very different kinds of models beside us and ahead of us. Ellen was trained when the contemporary women's movement was getting under way, but she was still one of only four women in her medical-school class. Joan matured in an earlier era of exploration and liberation, before World War II, and she had the images of Pavlova and Isadora Duncan and Martha Graham to inform her sense of possibility as a woman in the world of dance.

Because we are engaged in a day-by-day process of self-invention—not discovery, for what we search for does not exist until we find it—both the past and the future are raw material, shaped and reshaped by each individual. Four of us have close to half our adult lives still ahead. None has completed her story. My mother believed that all women, whether they have had busy multiple careers or are reviving old interests after decades as homemakers, have a hidden resource of energy and vitality for their later years. She called it "postmenopausal zest." Even Joan, who is in her eighties, may still do some of her most important work, because for the first time the significance of that work is being fully acknowledged. When we started work, she described the new book she was writing about wisdom and the senses. Before my book was finished, hers had appeared. Even as I was writing, she and Erik were moving from California to a joint household in Cambridge, and undertaking new kinds of teaching.

Each of the women whose lives are woven into this book is a woman of stature, but it is impossible to know how far their achievements will stretch in the future. When I started thinking about this project in 1984, I had major tasks to finish before I could begin, a memoir of my parents and my father's final book to complete, but I immediately started to think about the women I wanted to include. I made my selections one by one, but even as I proceeded, they were moving from strength to strength and becoming more public figures. When I began, Johnnetta was a professor; today she is a college president. There is no way to know what she will be able to contribute from that position to the improvement of education for blacks and women, indeed to the improvement of all American education. The focus of Ellen's work with the homeless has shifted from research to action, but it is not yet possible to guess how it will inform and shape sustained policy commitments. There is no way to tell whether Alice's work will become a technological landmark, flourish within a narrow and specific niche, or languish as technological directions change. The relationships and the circumstances of their lives also continue to evolve.

These are lives in flux, lives still indeterminate and subject to further discontinuities. This very quality protects me from the temptation to interpret them as pilgrimages to some fixed goal, for there is no way to know which fragments of the past will prove to be relevant in the future. Composing a life involves a continual reimagining of the future and reinterpretation of tl ⌐ past to give meaning to the present, remembering best those events that prefigured what followed, forgetting those that proved to have no meaning within the narrative.

Johnnetta described to me being taken to meet Maruca, a diviner in São Paulo, by a Brazilian anthropologist who had just written a doctoral dissertation on divination. Maruca is a woman in the service of the ancient Yoruba gods, the Orishas, brought by slaves from Nigeria.

"We got to this ordinary house in an ordinary working-class neighborhood. Maruca sat on the end of her bed, and there was a chair for me and a table, where I recognized all the things the Yoruba use for divination: a glass of water, a snake plant, the carved image of a fist to keep away the evil eye, the cowrie shells. Then I looked up at this woman, and she had the most penetrating eyes I had ever seen in my life. She asked my name and then she grabbed the cowries as if to throw them and went into some form of trance, acting as a medium rather than divining. She looked at me and said, 'You are about to change your job, to do something that is very close to what you now do but it's different and it's what very few women do in your country. It's a job working among our people, a very important job, and you must let the Orishas guide you.' Well, this was July, and I couldn't imagine what she was talking about. I'm not looking for a job! I teach anthropology at Hunter College. And I don't believe in divination! But then she went on to describe me in ways that had me sitting there bawling like a baby, because I confronted myself in the description. She talked about the pain I had gone through, particularly as I broke with my husband, and then she identified my Orishas, a male and a female, Ogun the warrior and Yansan, and said that she saw my life extended back in an unbroken line from West Africa." It was August 1 when Johnnetta got back to New York. When she walked into her office she found not one but several notes, each from a friend who had proposed her name to the newly announced search committee for the Spelman presidency. "And that," laughed Johnnetta, "is how Spelman College is connected to Brazil." An unbroken line of meaning that is also an unbroken line of commitment.

Alice, in her narratives about her evolving interest in management, kept going back to her final months at Harvard Observatory, when she worked on the design of experimental equipment for Skylab. She had declined an invitation to head the engineering group for the project because she was preoccupied with other emotional issues, and watched the project founder even though she was successful in her own technical assignment. "I was just treating the work as a sort of puzzle that I had to get solved, instead of thinking about the significance of the work for other people, so the project never came together. Harvard didn't fly an experiment on that satellite. They flew empty space. They sent up a lead box instead. That was traumatic for me, even though no one could point a finger at me because I wasn't in charge."

In the spring of my first year at Amherst College, a senior professor and alumnus came up to my husband at a cookout and told him warmly that I was doing "amazingly well" as dean. Even though the comment was intended benevolently, it was a reflection of the constant atmosphere of sexism at Amherst. Still, I took it as friendly and believed there was a real willingness to move beyond it. It is hard now not to see that comment as an omen of an unfolding sequence in which old assumptions were reasserted and habitual bias made me vulnerable. It's hard to remember the positive atmosphere at the time. So it is that many people only remember the good times with a beloved spouse who has died and only the painful moments in a marriage that has failed. We can often look at a grown-up child and find the threads of continuity, saying he or she was always a politician, a scientist, an artist.

We also edit the past to make it more intelligible in cultural terms. As memories blur, we supply details from a pool of general knowledge. With every retelling, words that barely fit begin to seem more appropriate as the meaning slips and slides to fit the stereotype. Was my English nanny as perfectly true to form as I remember her, or has the memory been smoothed and normalized? And what about the smoothing that denies the painful parts of happy memories and even makes nightmares more consistent? What about the inappropriate emotions denied and the anomalies that drop out of our storytelling? Even for the recent past and in situations where there would seem to be little motivation for distortion, memories are modified and details supplied to fit cultural expectations.

Women and men who pioneer new roles have a difficult time, for to the extent that their present defies cultural stereotypes, their past may be elusive, and yet too much forgetting can be a mistake, for any fragment of the past may prove to be important when a changed present makes new demands. When my husband and I were in Iran, I organized a cross-cultural research group on Iranian values, but I had great difficulty finding Iranian women who could play the double role involved, contributing both memory and analysis, social science and introspection. For the men in the group, the challenge of bridging the gap between early experience and training was rewarding; for the women, the chasm between socialization and mature roles was greater and harder to bridge. To remember what it was like to be a child, being prepared for traditional roles in Iranian society, and then to violate those roles by analytic discussion was too painful. There were women who were skilled and analytic scholars, but their childhood memories were blurred and remote; they had adjusted to dissonance by forgetting. There were also articulate traditional women who delighted in recalling the vivid details of their childhoods, but could not dissect or compare. American women who matured before the women's movement have the same kind of problem but to a lesser degree, for they have a far narrower chasm to bridge.

I have not tried to verify these narratives, beyond attending to issues of internal consistency and checking them against my knowledge of the individuals. The accounts as I heard them are themselves part of the process of composing lives. They are autobiographical, not biographical, shaped by each person's choice and selective memory and by the circumstances of our work together. No doubt they are shaped again by my own selections, resonating variously with my own experience. These are stories I have used to think with, sometimes quoting at length and sometimes very briefly, sometimes approaching an issue almost entirely through the eyes of one woman and at other times lining them all up for comparison.

Storytelling is fundamental to the human search for meaning, whether we tell tales of the creation of the earth or of our own early choices. Each of these women is engaged in inventing a new kind of story. Not only is it impossible to know what the future holds for them, it is impossible to know what their memories of the past will be when they bring them out again in the future, in some new and changed context.

The process of improvisation that goes into composing a life is compounded in the process of remembering a life, like a patchwork quilt in a watercolor painting, rumpled and evocative. Yet it is this second process, composing a life through memory as well as through day-to-day choices, that seems to me most essential to creative living. The past empowers the present, and the groping footsteps leading to this present mark the pathways to the future.

FROM STRENGTH
TO STRENGTH

JOAN AND ERIK MARRIED IN 1931 IN VIENNA, where he
was being trained by Anna Freud to be a child analyst. They
came to the United States in 1933 and moved to the West
Coast in 1939, where I first met them after the war. Erik
became more and more involved in research and writing in
addition to seeing patients, building on Freud's theories of
the origins of sexuality in childhood and the role of the ego
in the healthy personality. His theory of the life cycle focused
on the emergence of characteristic strengths through the
resolution of developmental crises, from infancy, when children struggle for trust and will, to old age, when the danger
is despair. During those years, Joan was raising her three
children, channeling her interests in the arts into projects

she organized for them and at their schools—children's art exhibits and Christmas pageants with real sheep for the shepherds. When her youngest, Sue, was ten, Joan enrolled herself and the children in a summer craft school and began learning the art and craft of jewelry making. Soon she was organizing an exchange among local craftspeople and establishing a regional arts center, a community context for individual creativity.

In 1951, the Eriksons moved to Stockbridge, Massachusetts, where Erik worked at the Austen Riggs Psychiatric Center, primarily with adolescent patients. It was there that he developed the concept for which he is still most widely known of a crisis of identity occurring in adolescence or young adulthood. During that period, Joan, who had always participated in his struggles with theory, began working with patients for the first time, organizing an activities program that acquired capital letters and became an essential part of the institution.

Joan is insistent that the Austen Riggs Activities Program is neither therapy nor entertainment. Not therapy, because the artists who work there do not interpret the symbolic meaning of patient work as therapists do, moving them toward explicit insight; instead they accept the work as valuable in its own right and help patients to develop their skills. Not entertainment, because the work provides a setting for addressing real tasks and accepting real challenges. Joan's view is that art, like life, is founded on different kinds of strength, and that troubled young people can discover and develop strengths as they meet the challenges of giving concrete expression to their imaginations. "There's a recapitulation of the stages of the life cycle whenever you go to do something, a picture for example. You have to have a certain basic trust that you can do this—you are going to do this. You have to have will, you have to have imagination enough and fancy enough to do it your way, to make it unique. You have to have confidence, identity, and so on."

An exploration of the ways women combine the materials of their lives must address this question of needed strengths, strength to imagine something new and strength to remain with it. For women moving out of traditional domesticity, creative energies are subverted not only by conflicting commitments but also by the steady drag of disparagement and prejudice pulling them toward the acceptance of subordinate roles. No one can expect, of course, to go through life without meeting discouragement and criticism, but every failure is more costly if it is accompanied by the implied message from outside, and the hidden belief within, that little more could have been expected. Those who move beyond discouragement are those who start out with a core of confidence and strength and who are lucky enough to continue to grow through environments that do not exploit the residual vulnerabilities everyone brings from childhood. All of the women I worked with on this project have had to deal with frustrations and with painful and costly choices and interruptions. Nevertheless, they have creatively reassembled the pieces again and again.

There are plenty of casualties in the developmental process. Sometimes whole groups fail to thrive, while other groups or individuals grow up with a firm confidence in their own value and potential for achievement, making more of their lives as a result. In America today, while some minority communities can pass on an expectation of success, large numbers of black children grow up relegated to an expendable underclass; they place as little value on themselves and their potential achievements as does the society. The same is true of many Hispanics and descendents of the white migrants of the Dust Bowl days, some of whom remain rootless farm workers two generations later, still disparaged as "Okies" by others and even by themselves. Children who know they have few options open to them may daydream of being astronauts or movie stars, but nowhere in the dream is there a realistic and realistically imagined next step. Women also are only now beginning to break free of an ingrained and disabling sense of inferiority rooted in assumptions about the options available to them.

Joan spoke one day about how she had arrived at her own clear identity as a dancer, an identity that has continued whether she has been able to dance or not. She was in New Jersey, studying to be an instructor in physical education. "I always had wished to be a dancer, I mean I thought that would be it, that would be the thing that would be wonderful. But I never thought of myself as a dancer. I was an athlete, and *husky*." Joan laughed warmly and lightly as she often did when our conversations touched on something that must have been painful long ago. "In those days, dancers were teensy, and petite, and appropriately light and little and all of that, which I wasn't; at least I thought that compared to them I was an elephant. It just was like those visions of something fine that seems entirely inappropriate, like wishing you were an opera star or something. Then this dance teacher from Barnard came over to the normal school where I was, and she was quite a husky babe, you know, she was no little delicate spring flower. She was very light on her feet, but she was at least as tall as I was, and I was always tremendously tall. And I watched her move around, and I thought, well, you're no bigger than she is, maybe you've got what it takes. Her name was Mary O'Donnell. I'll never forget. So I began really taking my dancing seriously, and after a while I began to be commended, I mean I was doing good. I think it was toward the end of that year when I really latched on and I said, Boy! That's it. That's what I am. I'm a dancer. I just knew it like that. And after that everything was just sheer bliss that I had to do."

All five of us were fortunate in our beginnings, yet all of us have had experiences that undermined confidence and aspiration. The assumptions made about women and girls when we were children, which still linger today, are bound to leave wounds. Prosperity is not sufficient to remove these problems. The daughters of successful fathers may indeed incorporate that achievement into their image of themselves, but they may equally well receive the message that achievement is not for girls. Devoted care is also not sufficient. Most women today have grown up with mothers who, for all their care and labor, were regarded as having achieved little. Women with a deep desire to be like their mothers are often faced with the choice between accepting a beloved image that carries connotations of inferiority and dependency or rejecting it and thereby losing an important sense of closeness.

I believe the issue of female inferiority still arises for

virtually every woman growing up in this society. I grew up in an environment where no one told me females were inferior or that significant achievement would necessarily be beyond my reach, but the belief was all around me. The departures of both my parents for long periods of war work when I was very little must have made me question my value and importance—their work came first. Somehow I merged that idiosyncratic experience with the culturally supported attitude toward women. As a young woman, I never questioned the assumption that when I married what I could do would take second place to what my husband could do. Twenty-five years later, I have slighted my own value so often that it is hard to learn to take it seriously. Instead, I get things done by finding rationales for valuing the task and then sacrificing myself for it. And all of this is available as a bad model for the next generation.

These attitudes show up again and again in the texture of everyday life. For at least twenty years, whenever I interrupted my husband when he was busy, he finished what he was doing before he responded. When he interrupted me, I would drop what I was doing to respond to him, automatically giving his concerns priority. As time passed, I learned occasionally to say please let me finish here first, but usually this has made me so uncomfortable that my concentration has been lost. By now, Barkev has learned that both of us need to be on guard against my willingness to sacrifice my time and my space, as if my goals were automatically less important than those of other members of the family. Yet we have all benefited from my peripheral vision.

If women were brought up to be more centered on

themselves, many of the conflicts and discontinuities that disrupt their lives would be irrelevant, peripheral to the central definition of self. They could move from context to context without a painful sense of contingency, but to do so might involve a loss of awareness, a narrowing of attention. To be effectively centered is to affirm the existence of an internal gyroscope, to believe of oneself that *plus ça change, plus c'est la même chose.* Attaining such a conviction is difficult and painful for women who have always been encouraged to bend to exterior winds. This is why an affirmation of continuity among various stages and commitments is such a central strength. Even the continuity of self-sacrifice and dependency can be used to bridge painful discontinuities. Women who can maintain their roles of wife and mother may adjust better than their men to the loss of a family farm or to becoming refugees. The ideal is to be both centered and sensitive.

Ellen grew up in a Jewish family in New York, the second of four sisters, her mother a full-time homemaker and her father a lawyer. She never had to give way to brothers, but she has always been torn between preparing for achievement and the attraction of her mother's model. Ellen has especially wanted to give her children the kind of home life she had as a child. Her early ambition was to be a lawyer like her father, or a judge. Later, when she was at Brandeis University, her ambition shifted to psychology, because of a family friend working with autistic children, and then to psychiatry.

Any minority status carries ambivalent overtones, but Ellen's Jewish background has been a source of strength. The notion of a chosen people includes the sense that divine choice is a burden, bringing an inevitability of suffering, but still the sense of specialness is there. This specialness has often been amplified, for the Jewish emphasis on knowledge of the law has meant that Jewish communities historically had exceptionally high levels of literacy compared to the European peasant communities in which they lived. Thus, although the Jewish people have often been at a social and economic disadvantage, this has not, on the whole, produced a sense of inferiority but rather a distinctive and tenacious confidence. We see a similar phenomenon in the rapid success of immigrants from the Far East, many of whom arrive in America penniless but who come from groups long convinced of the superiority of their stock and civilization.

In contrast, Johnnetta comes from a community that has had the suspicion of inferiority and the sense of contingency ground into it. Johnnetta grew up in Jacksonville, at a time when Florida was very much more a part of the Deep South than it is now, and the South as a whole was deeper in its Jim-Crow tradition. Still, because of a family insurance business, her family had the respect of the black community and even of the white community. When she went to downtown stores and banks, even white people would know she was Abraham Lincoln Lewis's granddaughter, and all through her childhood, the phone would ring at night, calling her father out to help get someone out of jail. He acted as a liaison in other ways, representing the black community in the rationing administration during the war. Johnnetta's Lewis relatives owned houses at the seashore—at American Beach, which had been developed by the Afro-American Life Insurance Company and was the only stretch of beach open to black people at that time in the entire state of Florida. As an adult, Johnnetta has benefited from programs designed to bring Afro-Americans and women into fuller participation, but she never doubted her own merits as a result. She grew up knowing she was smart.

Still, this sense of specialness had its limits. In Jacksonville, it was impossible to be unaware of the parks and clubs and beaches that were closed to anyone of color. Exclusion and the awareness of a world denied began at the front door, for residential segregation was not as sharp in the traditional South as it has become in northern cities with their huge, all-black ghetto neighborhoods. The universal childhood experience of being warned to go to the toilet before going out was framed by the reminder that restrooms open to a black child were few and far between. As a child, Johnnetta had fantasies whenever the family went out of town in a car at night that the car would break down and the Klan would come. She would pray that her father, a Mason, would be able to rescue them by giving some magic sign that would be recognized by a white Klansman who was also a Mason.

"I found out about race very early. I have a recollection from when I was three or four years old of a kid calling me nigger." I asked her how she knew "nigger" was a bad word. "The tone of voice," she retorted, provoked by the question, "and the rocks that are being thrown—they tell you that 'nigger' is an insult.

"Very early on," she continued, shifting to an analytical tone, "black kids are told as a means of cushioning or protecting, or they come and say why are they calling me that? I think it's very common for black parents to try to protect,

43

to give those early years of warmth and love without the lessons that one is gonna shortly learn. I would argue that there are few black folk that do not remember the first time. The reason for taking such a term and making it a term of endearment is to soften the intensity of that pain, so 'my main nigger' becomes 'my best friend.' It's compensatory because it is so very very painful.

"I remember always having to wait in stores and thinking that was so unfair, I got there first, why was I having to wait? And if the salespeople weren't kin, why were they calling the black folk 'auntie' and 'uncle'? I just remember thinking that white people really ought to cool it—that this was ridiculous."

Johnnetta was sharply conscious of race as a child in the South, but like most of us before the contemporary women's movement, she was largely unaware that being female can be just as much of a disadvantage as being black. "You've got to get out of the household at least for a moment to meet up with the race question, but you wake up every day meeting the gender question, so you don't even notice it. It's pretty intimate.

"I remember looking up at the white faces in the stained-glass windows and thinking, all these people down here are black. Much later on in the black-power movement, it wasn't hard to think back that in Sunday School I would sing, 'And Jesus will wash me whiter than snow.' But I never remember raising the question that Jesus was male and so was God. That never occurred to me as a kid. I also remember thinking that I certainly should not be raising questions about was there a God. Sumpin' prob'ly be comin' in zap me any minute!" Johnnetta plays fluently between different speech styles, ringing the changes between the southern black English of her childhood and the formal academic style of the northern universities where she has spent most of her life.

Johnnetta only became aware of gender issues and the complex relationship between gender and race at the end of the struggles of the sixties, partly because gender differences take a different form in the black community, partly because the race issue seemed more urgent. In Johnnetta's childhood, all the women she knew worked, including her mother, who taught English and was registrar at a small church-affiliated black school called Edward Waters College. Johnnetta only started thinking seriously about gender on her first visit to Cuba.

"There I was, seeing for the first time the possibility that the race thing was not forever and ever; and then the other -ism was right up there saying, what about me? Then of course came the real whammy, that dealing with sexism is far more difficult. It's gonna be one that takes us longer as a species than almost any other. How early we socialize about this stuff—and how intimately!"

She went to Cuba with a delegation of Afro-Americans who were highly sensitized to issues of color. Wherever they went, they asked how many blacks there were (on the hospital staff, in the university, and so on), deeply suspicious when no one seemed willing to answer. Finally they realized that Cubans, while aware of shades of complexion, simply do not organize society in terms of color (particularly not the empirically nonsensical black and white of North American society). Johnnetta had simply not believed in the possibility of a society not stratified by race. But at every turn in Cuba, she was sharply reminded that the society was still organized on gender lines and that postrevolutionary Cuba was dominated by old-fashioned patriarchy and Latin American machismo, which the government has only started to address seriously in the last few years.

"Another thing is where racism and sexism are reproduced. You can zap racism a lot easier because you have it expressed behaviorally in the public square. There's no need to express racism behaviorally in the household cause you're not gonna have none o' *them* people in there with you, OK? But you got women in that household with you and that's why at the very beginning you are reproducing that stuff. A perfect example is what happens in Cuba now on the gender question. These young junior-high-school kids go off to the schools in the countryside, and there is a great deal of equality. The girls, if anything, are outshining the boys academically, and the boys have to clean the school just like the girls do. And then they go back home at the end of two weeks, and they are right back in that household with Daddy waiting to be served his *cafecito* and Momma doin' all the double-shift work. So unless the state is gonna extend its arm into that household, it's just a lot harder to deal with all that stuff."

In trying to think about the strengths with which we began, I was struck by the advantages that some of us had, mothers who had achieved as much or more than our fathers without having given up the chance to marry and have children. We also did most of our growing up without competing brothers on the scene who might have been put in an implicit position of superiority.

Alice was an only child until she was ten, when her younger brother was born. Her mother was a teacher of mathematics and her father a physicist, getting a second doctorate in mathematics. Although her mother was not her primary intellectual model, Alice did grow up with a love for math, and she never acquired the expectation of being unable to do math that seems to be critical in keeping girls out of science. The family was in Rumania during the war, and then they lived in Paris for five years. When Alice came to the United States, the family went through long periods of poverty when her father was unemployed. Still, she had the immediate experience of being better schooled and culturally more sophisticated than her agemates, which may have protected her against the tug of conformity. No one seems to have instructed her to fail until the end of high school. She had won the highest regional scores in a Grumman Aircraft competition for a scholarship to engineering school. After an interview in which she admitted to an interest in art and music as well as engineering, she was told kindly that she would not get the scholarship because she was a girl and she had too many other interests. By that time, Alice had enough confidence in her own direction to be angry rather than discouraged. "I was a bit bullshit. I thought, I wouldn't want to work for your company anyway. But I was still going to do aeronautics, because I thought airplanes were wonderful. I spent a summer doing flutter analysis, but what was really exciting to me was not the offices, but the factory floor where the airplanes were assembled." Alice went on to MIT and left after getting her degree because she wanted practical experience.

There is a sense in which my story echoes Alice's, for I too was an only child with a partial experience of siblings: half siblings born later and perennial playmates. From the public and contemporary point of view, my mother was far more successful than my father, whose career was filled with frustrations. Today, the value of his work is still being discovered, and more of my time goes to a continuing dialogue with his ideas. I grew up admiring him and worrying about him, as Alice worried about her father when his career faltered after he came to the United States.

It was critical for me that both my parents treated me with respect, giving me real tasks and sitting down and having serious conversations. Alice remembers feeling very clearly that she should take charge when she and her mother were fleeing to Paris before the Russian advance into Rumania. "Even though she was the grownup, I felt I understood things much better. And then in Paris, our friends were wonderful, scientists and writers and painters, and the most wonderful thing was that I was invited to all of the soirees, and I was not babied. All the grownups liked me and would talk about anything. In France, when you start to read you don't read Dick and Jane, you start with excerpts from Molière, Racine, Corneille, excerpts from all the great writers, so you feel comfortable participating in any conversation about serious literature. And my mother was a wonderful mother. She took me to plays and operas and parks and made sure I had a wonderful experience and talked to me seriously." Because women are so often treated like children, it is important that memories of childhood be memories of respect and confidence.

Time was another resource that some of us garnered early on. When I interviewed Ellen, I was intrigued to hear that she had finished medical school when she was twenty-three, since I have always been aware of my good fortune in having gotten my Ph.D. at the same age. Johnnetta started college at fifteen as a result of a special talent search among black teenagers. Each of us then has had a hidden chronological resource, an edge of two or three years to draw on when the facts of being female pulled us back. I used that edge, created by rushing through my education, when my husband's choices meant I had to make repeated fresh starts on my career; Johnnetta used hers on long delays in finishing the writing of a doctoral thesis while she had two young children on her hands, born after the research was done; Ellen became professionally established before her age group, so that she was able at a later date to reduce her professional commitments for motherhood without dropping out.

Each of us was once ahead of the game. Although we aren't allowed to keep our lead in this particular handicap race, no one would be able to say our educations were wasted. Still, one of the ironies in all these lives is that the things traditionally said to girls when they spoke of career aspirations—you will just get married and have a baby—do have a degree of validity. None of these women abandoned work entirely, but the issues of intimacy and nurturance are woven into their achievements, which thus become harder to recognize.

Joan realized quite early that she was more interested in dance as education than as performance and that she would work with children instead of young adults. "Their posture was so bad and their shoes were awful and they wore bloomers still, the way I did. You were all fretted up with stuff that kept you from moving freely. I didn't want to spend my time doing remedial gymnastics. I knew what those bodies looked like and how terrible their whole feeling was. So I had decided I would work with children and keep them from being deformed, and they might be able to maintain that when they grew older."

As a result, Joan decided to do a dissertation on the teaching of dance in Europe and tried to find research funding. "I remember going to one guy at Columbia who was kind of a friend and advisor, and saying I wanted to do this, and he just laughed and said, 'You know, you girls that go off and want to do these things, it's just a joke. You'll get married and then you'll never come back. We can't waste money on you!' I said, 'No such thing! I'll go on with this whatever I do.'"

She didn't get a grant, even in that field that was already in many ways led by women. But she went to Europe anyway, did her research, and wrote a first draft of a dissertation. She did get married and did not return to Columbia or finish the doctorate. And yet the clarity of her commitment to dance and dance education was never abandoned and has been woven into emerging understandings of how children develop and how the sick are healed, and today even that research may be recycled.

We all married quite early, either as students or soon after, in ways that fit with our other interests. None of us expected to give up our other work and involvements completely, but we had rather limited understandings of the puzzle this posed. We all put the puzzle together differently. Two of us, Joan and Johnnetta, had children early, setting our work aside; Ellen and I deferred childbearing until we were professionally established. Alice has been in many ways the least domestic of us all and has never had children. After finishing at MIT, she took a job in R&D at General Electric in Utica, which gave her a chance to develop real, practical competence in engineering; she expected that she would eventually return to school for a doctorate in theory. "Coming out of MIT I didn't have the sense of hardware I learned later. But I did learn how to think theoretically there, not just plugging in formulae." She did a theoretical senior thesis in hydrodynamics and electromagnetism, looking at the energy not accounted for in the rotation of the earth due to the movement of fluids inside. It concerned issues of shortening relative distance and changing the frame of reference, so she used the example of an infinite rake in a garden and asked how fast a caterpillar would have to move to escape.

"I was looking for that person who was a brilliant scientist who could also listen to music or look at a painting," Alice remembers, "so the world of people I could be involved with was rather small—I guess I just didn't think much about sexual drives because my head drive was so strong that it dominated everything. But then a French woman I had been very close to at MIT who had moved to New York was killed in a fatal car accident, and I went into total shock. All at once I realized I would never see this woman whom I loved again, and I had never taken the time to go and see her. And then I suddenly got involved with a lot of men, and it was all very exciting and very draining. I really can't figure out how I survived except that when I worked on technical things I worked as if nothing else was going on—but the rest was chaos." That period ended in exhausted collapse combined with a toxic reaction to an over-the-counter sleeping pill.

After that, Alice spent a few weeks with her parents and went back to Utica to marry Paul, an artist and industrial designer. Even many years after their divorce, he continued to be a steadying and supportive friend. "He was extraordinarily original, one of the few artists I've known who could talk and who really loved technology. Theoretical science came more easily to me—I could see how to put things together and make them work as easily as he could pick up a paintbrush and out comes this beautiful thing, and I'd say, what difference does it make if I do it with a differential equation and you don't? Don't get bent out of shape."

The couple soon moved back to the Boston area. Except for a brief period of attempted collaboration with her father, Alice went through the early years of her scientific and engineering career working under the umbrella of large institutions and avoiding leadership roles, motivated by the sheer pleasure of the technical work. It was only as an expression of caring for her lover Jack and, after his death, for the continuity of their engineering work together, and for the people who had depended on it, that she eventually accepted leadership responsibility. "There I was," she said, "a person who had previously been used to doing technology, where the only condition of doing interesting work was proving I could do it. I had never asked for anything other people wanted, money, power, all I wanted to do was solve problems and then find another problem."

No one acts entirely out of self-interest, just as no one acts entirely out of altruism, but the assumption of self-interest is a common simplification in attempts to understand the behavior of others, particularly for those whose good sense has been diluted by reading too much economics. Women often err in the opposite direction. Because they were traditionally taught to emphasize service, their choices may be unintelligible and therefore deeply suspect. Yet although their motives don't match the expectations of those around them, I have been struck by how terribly hard this group of women worked as students and later on in their careers, and how often work is unappreciated when the motive behind it is not understood.

It is not only in childhood that people of high potential can be encouraged or held back and their promise subverted or sustained. The year before I went to Amherst, a group of women had declined to stand for tenure. One of them simply said that after six years she was used up, too weary and too eroded by constant belittlement to accept tenure if it were offered to her. Women were worn down or burnt out. During the three years I spent as dean of the faculty, as I watched some young faculty members flourish and others falter, I gradually realized that the principal instrument of sexism was not the refusal to appoint women or even the refusal to promote (though both occurred, for minorities as well as women), but the habit of hiring women and then dealing with them in such a way that when the time came for promotion it would be reasonable to deny it. It was not hard to show that a particular individual who was a star in graduate school had somehow belied her promise, had proved unable to achieve up to her potential.

This subversion was accomplished by taking advantage of two kinds of vulnerability that women raised in our society tend to have. The first is the quality of self-sacrifice, a learned willingness to set their own interests aside and be used and even used up by the community. Many women at Amherst ended up investing vast amounts of time in needed public-service activities, committee work, and teaching nondepartmental courses. Since these activities were not weighed significantly in promotion decisions, they were self-destructive.

The second kind of vulnerability trained into women is a readiness to believe messages of disdain and derogation. Even women who arrived at Amherst full of confidence gradually became vulnerable to distorted visions of themselves, no longer secure that their sense of who they were matched the perceptions of others. When a new president, appointed in 1983, told me before coming and without previous discussion with me that he had heard I was "consistently confrontational," that I had made Amherst "a tense, unhappy place," and that he would want to select a new dean, I should have reacted to his picture of me as bizarre, and indeed confronted its inaccuracy, but instead I was shattered. It took me a year to understand that he was simply accepting the semantics of senior men who expected a female dean to be easily disparaged and bullied, like so many of the young women they had managed to dislodge. It took me a year to recover a sense of myself as worth defending and to learn to be angry both for myself and for the college as I watched a tranquil campus turned into one that was truly tense and unhappy.

The problem, as I came to understand it when I had had time to follow the development of individuals over several years, was not only to ensure the hiring of women and minority members. This was hard enough to do from the dean's office, but what was even harder was to turn Amherst College into a place where all young men and women hired to teach (as well as all students) could thrive, whether they were promoted and asked to stay on or not, a place where whatever talents and strengths they brought from childhood could be fostered and they could go from strength to strength. Such a place would have to be challenging as well as supportive, like Joan's Activities Program at Austen Riggs, providing room for criticism and discipline as well as indulgence. But it could not be belittling.

The need to sustain human growth should be a matter of concern for the entire society, even more fundamental than the problem of sustaining productivity. This, surely, is the deepest sense of homemaking, whether in a factory or a college or a household. For all of us, continuing development depends on nurture and guidance long after the years of formal education, just as it depends on seeing others ahead on the road with whom it is possible to identify. A special effort is needed when doubts have been deeply implanted during the years of growing up or when some fact of difference raises barriers or undermines those identifications, but all of us are at risk, not only through childhood but through all the unfolding experiences of life that present new problems and require new learning. Education, whether for success or failure, is never finished. Building and sustaining the settings in which individuals can grow and unfold, not "kept in their place" but empowered to become all they can be, is not only the task of parents and teachers, but the basis of management and political leadership—and simple friendship.

OPENING
TO THE WORLD

HUMAN BEINGS TEND to regard the conventions of their own societies as natural, often as sacred. One of the great steps forward in history was learning to regard those who spoke odd-sounding languages and had different smells and habits as fully human, as similar to oneself. The next step from this realization, the step which we have still not fully made, is the willingness to question and purposefully alter one's own conditions and habits, to learn by observing others. If a particular arrangement is not necessary, it might be possible to choose to change it. Still, aristocratic Chinese ladies of the old regime, crippled for life by the binding of their feet, looked down on peasant women with unbound feet. Exposure to other ways of doing things is insufficient if it is not combined with empathy and respect.

I grew up a beneficiary of openness to alternatives of belief and custom. All four of my grandparents were atheists, which meant that they had dissented from beliefs taken for granted by those around them, living lives of conscious choice. For my mother and later for me, taking an interest in religion was rather venturesome, involving the notion that belief is not a given of growing up in a particular family but a matter of choice. In some ways, my grandparents were chauvinistic about their chosen nonconformities and felt rather superior to those who had less education or enlightenment. But in other ways, I see them as open to the imagination of alternative ways of being.

My father's father, who crusaded ferociously for his convictions against various kinds of spiritualism and Lamarckianism, thought of his own vocation of scientist as lofty but lower than that of artist. He collected the paintings and drawings of William Blake, Japanese prints, embroideries and old-master drawings. As I see them now, these are very different choices. To collect old-master drawings was to choose an economical and attainable form of a familiar excellence, but to immerse himself in the visions and prophetic writings of Blake was to embrace a different consciousness— bizarre, angry, and strangely beautiful, turning ordinary perceptions upside down. "The harlot's cry from street to street/Will weave old England's winding sheet." I have wondered occasionally, in these years when we have learned to look anew at needlework as forms of women's expression, whether the embroideries he collected were also ways to enter other modes of thinking and being, especially since his mother, his wife, and his sisters were all variously involved in women's rights and in exploring new roles.

When my mother wrote about her childhood, it always seemed that her chosen model was her paternal grandmother, but recently I have become increasingly curious about her mother, my maternal grandmother. Richard Juliani, a sociologist studying the history of Italians in America, has pointed out that Margaret Mead first learned about the importance of culture from her mother's research on Italian immigrants. Long before she encountered anthropology and went to Samoa, she had done fieldwork with her mother in New Jersey, where she met and learned to respect people with different customs. She had heard her mother's convictions on the human capacity to change and adapt; she had also heard her counter the arguments of the eugenics movement, which maintained that Italian and Eastern European immigrants were genetically inferior.

For Americans today, composing a life means integrating one's own commitments with the differences created by change and the differences that exist between the peoples of the world with whom we increasingly come into contact. Because we have an altered sense of the possible, every choice has a new meaning.

When Johnnetta was growing up, a nonracist America was hardly imaginable; today it can be imagined but must still be struggled for. The imagination of difference was also blocked in another way, for educated black people in Jacksonville looked down on black people from the Caribbean and Africa. The implication was that blacks in Jacksonville should aspire to be like the white people around them, but there was a secondary message beating on them that they would always be something less.

"I remember all those derogatory terms. 'Monkey chasers' were the people from the Caribbean. Because of the closeness of Florida to the Bahamas, Jamaica, Barbados, there was a lot of that sentiment. In my family, we were told not to have that view, that black people from other places were not less good than black people born in the U.S. My great-grandfather had named his company the *Afro-American Life Insurance Company*, after all. But even so, if I wanted a dress that my mother thought was too red, she'd say, 'You don't want to look like some . . .' (she'd use a distorted set of syllables supposed to indicate some African tribe), 'You don't want to look like one of those Ubidubi tribes.' There were conflicting messages about 'those tribal jump-up-and-down-big-lipped people' that you didn't want to have any part of."

Black consciousness has not only affirmed a positive and equal identity for American blacks, but it has also offered a sense of multiple possibilities: Africa as a place of rich and fertile variation, experiments in kingship as old as Solomon, herders and farmers and hunters and sculptors; Brazil and Cuba and Haiti, with recurrent themes but profound differences. Johnnetta speaks of drawing on her background in anthropology to bring sisters from throughout the lands of the African diaspora to Spelman College to affirm and proclaim that there is more than one way of being black, just as there is more than one way of being female. This, for her, is education for choice. When you talk to her about what she hopes to achieve, she returns again and again to the idea that Afro-Americans and women need to discover their own diversity and in that discovery be freed from the notion that there is only a single possible direction of aspiration. "I'm on the case of the white folk about diversity, but I also think that Spelman has that responsibility. And by diversity, I mean to go beyond self. One of the ways that can happen is to have a community of students who are black women from other parts of the world. Who says that here at an all-black women's school we don't have to be concerned about diversity? You can't argue that there is insight and strength to be gained from diversity over there but you don't need it over here! But I don't think the two issues are mirror images, either."

Aspiration is elusive without models to aspire to, but following a single model has its own dangers. The son of a physician growing up in the suburbs can aspire to be like his father and close his eyes to the evidence that his life will necessarily be different. The daughter of a business executive can aspire to be like her father and understand that such an aspiration depends on change in the society, but she may still be the captive of a single vision of excellence. It was still hard, when Ellen went to medical school, for women to become physicians; beyond that, it was necessary for them to become a different kind of physician, to reshape the existing role. There has been a recurring debate in the women's movement between those who fought for the chance for middle-class white women to be like middle-class white men and those who affirm the many ways of being female, the needs and problems of other kinds of women, and the need for freedom for men and women to move in different directions. For some of us, "chauvinism" is simply a shortening of "male chauvinism." For others, it is a reminder of the dangers of devotion to the superiority of any group, gender, race, religion, or nation, or even to the truths of any era.

The real challenge comes from the realization of multiple alternatives and the invention of new models. Aspiration ceases to be a one-way street—from child to adult, from female inferiority to male privilege, from exclusion to full membership—and instead becomes open in all directions, claiming the possibility of inclusion and setting an individual course among the many ways of being human. Even this is not an adequate phrasing, because it suggests the possibility of choosing an existing model and following it toward a defined goal. The real challenge lies in assembling something new.

There are no singular models, but only resources for creative imagination. Many people grew up seeing my mother as a model, which is fine and helpful from a distance, but it would have been a mistake for me to try to be too much like her. I am like Ellen with her housewife mother: loving and determined to be different. At the same time, you cannot put together a life willy-nilly from odds and ends. Even in a crazy quilt, the various pieces, wherever they come from, have to be trimmed and shaped and arranged so they fit together, then firmly sewn to last through time and keep out the cold. Most quilts are more ambitious: they involve the imposition of a new pattern. But even crazy quilts are sewn against a backing; the basic sense of continuity allows improvisation. Composing a life involves an openness to possibilities and the capacity to put them together in a way that is structurally sound.

It had not occurred to me how much the capacity to combine new roles to create an innovative and integrated whole might depend on exposure to another culture. I knew, of course, that membership in a minority always involves an awareness of difference, but that is only a first step. Belonging to a minority group, especially when that membership is associated with poverty and limited education, may foster a lack of self-respect and a lack of the confidence to draw purposefully on one's own background. This has been true for the children of immigrants when their parents came from the very bottom of their own societies—Irish peasants fleeing from famine, Chinese coolies imported to work on the railroads, poor Sicilian farmers.

Johnnetta's way of looking at cultural alternatives is partly based on the paradoxical experience of being an advantaged member of a disadvantaged minority and partly based on her training and her travels as an anthropologist. She was captured for anthropology during her first year at Oberlin by George Eaton Simpson, who taught a class on racial and cultural minorities. "He put on a record of Jamaican music and right there in front of the class, he started to hyperventilate." Watching a white man not only talk about a part of black culture, but submit, in that moment in the classroom, to its eloquence, she grasped the idea that one could study culture, one's own or that of others, truly attending to it rather than using the stance of an observer as a way to dominate. Her willingness to look outward began from an altered way of looking at her own tradition.

The idea of an anthropology major was far from welcome back in Jacksonville. Johnnetta's grandfather, Papa, laughed at her. "I told Papa I was going to be an anthropologist, he asked me what that was, and I described it. He said, 'That's the craziest thing I've ever heard, you couldn't feed yourself,' and I cried. And then I remember my mother comforting me and saying that was exactly what I should go on to be: 'You have to do what you have to do.' But Papa's attitude was that I would go into the insurance business." Later on Johnnetta nearly married a man involved in a different black insurance company, but eventually she married Robert Cole, a white fellow student at Northwestern. "You went exogamous," I said, using the anthropological term for marriage outside of one's own kin group or tribe. Then it occurred to me, "No—that was another kind of endogamy, part of your new academic tribe."

Ellen too had ventured outside her own culture. She traced her concern with the problem of homelessness to a summer project in Africa when, for the first time, she had looked at illness as a societal rather than an individual problem. She went as part of a program for medical students sponsored by the Experiment in International Living, doing a survey of tuberculosis in western Nigeria. "The prevalence of TB was astounding, and not just pulmonary TB but kinds of TB that invade the other organs. I remember going to clinics for Pott's disease, which is tuberculosis of the spine. It's horrible. You don't see disease like that in this country. And the lifespan is short. People are just riddled with curable infectious diseases and parasites. Schistosomiasis, which is probably the number-one killer in the world, is rampant in that area. We tested a population of school-age children out in the bush, and I think we found about a third of the kids had it. It's a horrible disease. And I spent time in leper colonies. I think that experience really spun my head around. And also, it was the first time that I had traveled to a faraway place by myself. It was a very adventuresome trip, because—I mean, we were, as you can imagine, in a very primitive part of the world. I came back with some minor parasites and some side effects from the—I came back sick, basically.

"Then I went back to medical school after this very exciting and also very scary trip, really unsure about whether I wanted to be a doctor, whether I wanted all this responsibility. Here was a population just full of tuberculosis, which is a disease you can do something about, and they weren't even providing treatment. I was ready to go into one of my crusades and beat the bureaucrats over the head, but when you are in a foreign culture your hands are tied. I remember seeing someone dying of rabies and they weren't even medicating him, because medicine was so scarce it was saved for those who had a chance of surviving. It was my first exposure to a really horrifying systems problem. There's curable disease out there, and it's just not being treated."

In Africa, Ellen's vision had broadened to include the social context of disease. This prefigured a shift of focus from treating individual patients toward designing public-health strategies to help large numbers of people. In order to develop treatment or prevention strategies for a particular population, it is necessary first to learn to see them and then to become sufficiently visionary to imagine that their lives might be different. There is a whole structure of assumptions that must be overcome. Even before she became involved with the homeless, Ellen was involved in opening one of the first rape crisis centers located in the emergency ward of a general hospital. Rape too is a problem that could only be addressed when it became visible and when women began to realize that it was not a matter of individuals "asking for it" but of the way the society is organized—and to realize that the problem could be addressed systemically.

In Iran, I did some research and writing about American women who had married Iranian men and come to live in Iran. Many were intolerant of Iranian culture, learning little and struggling to replicate their lives in America. Others tried to assimilate completely, as Americans tend to expect immigrants to this country to do, and they only developed a capacity for true selection when their total embrace of their husbands' culture proved to be less than ideal. It is not sufficient to reject one tradition and embrace another—this is the convert's danger, involving an oversimplification of both. It is also not sufficient to camp out in a new tradition without commitment, taking refuge in relativism to avoid responsibility and using distance to avoid the need to criticize the culture one comes from.

Women have traditionally been regarded as conservative and inclined to stay at home. Going forth to seek adventure has been regarded as a male specialty—running away to sea, joining the circus, seeking new worlds to conquer. But conquest is not the best route to learning. An encounter with other cultures can lead to openness only if you can suspend the assumption of superiority, not seeing new worlds to conquer, but new worlds to respect. When young women arrived in Iran as the American wives of Iranian Muslims, they often came with assumptions of superiority, but their actual positions required sensitivity and adaptation, more like adopted children than like explorers arriving to claim new territory.

Ironically, patriarchal society in its most traditional forms often assumes a greater degree of adaptability in women than in men, because of the set of conventions referred to as patrilocality: men inherit property and status. A man can stay at home to assume the position occupied by his father, bringing in a young bride who is expected to adapt to a new environment. Often, of course, the home the bride leaves is just down the road. In Iran and throughout the Middle East, the tradition that a woman leaves her family and becomes a part of her husband's family is moderated by making the marriage as endogamous as possible. There is a strong preference for marriages between the children of brothers ("We wouldn't give our daughter to strangers," parents say). Still, it is the bride who is uprooted. "Whither thou goest I will go; and where thou lodgest I will lodge; thy people shall be my people, and thy God my God," Ruth says in the Bible (Ruth 1:16). She says it, as a widow, to her mother-in-law, Naomi. It is an expression not of individual friendship between two women but of the fact that a woman becomes a member of her husband's family, no longer of her own. Ruth's alternative was to go back to her family of origin in the hope of remarrying and becoming a member of still another family. Naomi had proposed that alternative to both her widowed daughters-in-law: "The

Lord grant that ye may find rest, each of you in the house of her husband" (Ruth 1:9).

Of all the foreign brides I knew in Iran, my most vivid memories are of a woman named Julia Samii, who was killed in a light-plane crash before the revolution. When I met her, she had lived in Iran for many years and had achieved a unique combination of the two cultures. Her husband was from one of the largest and most influential families of the Caspian region, and she had learned to move effectively within the extended family—in fact, she was one of the few foreign wives I knew who had learned to feel enriched rather than burdened by a multitude of relatives. Her children were all genuinely bicultural. She was a devout Catholic, going several times a week to early mass at St. Abraham's, a church run by Irish Dominicans that celebrated Abraham as the father of three often-conflicting faiths. The rest of the day, she worked for the Iranian Society for the Deaf, promoting the development of an Iranian sign language, work that brought her into contact with different levels of society and required a detailed knowledge of the culture as well as a commitment to change. I remember she once described to me the creation of a sign to represent the Persian word *khastegari,* the formal courtship in which the groom pays a series of visits to the home of a potential bride. The proposed sign was a crooked and beckoning finger, followed by a gesture of putting on a ring; Julia had successfully advocated a different sign, the peremptory beckoning replaced by hands on the heart.

As a young woman, I was uncomfortable with the marriage customs of my own tribe and with the multiple divorces of my parents, so I "married out" after a year of living in Israel in my first extended experience of another culture. Barkev was born in Syria, but his cultural tradition is Armenian. Unlike Johnnetta's husband Robert, Barkev came from outside my academic community. He had been an engineering student at Northeastern and later a student at the Harvard Business School, the place we used to call "the other side of the river." I learned to speak and write Armenian and to cook Armenian food, and Barkev became a social scientist. Both of our families were supportive, unlike Johnnetta and Robert's families. They were breaking much more explicit taboos. "My God, what am I gonna tell my mom," Johnnetta remembered thinking. "It's not just that he's white, the man's a radical!"

"One of my strongest recollections," she continued, "is the night when Robert Cole drove to Jacksonville to meet my mom. Somehow it was known—we've never been able to figure it out other than wiretapping of our phone—that Robert was coming. The threats began—that the Afro would be bombed, that someone in our family was gonna suffer—anonymous phone calls, voices that seemed white. That night my head hurt so bad I went to sleep and said wake me up when he comes. I woke up next morning to find I had slept through his arrival. My mother and Robert had found a bottle of scotch, and in the course of killing it they decided they could live with each other, though following that my mother decided it was more than she could ask me to take on and asked me not to marry him. We were being pressured from both sides. Up till the night before, I thought my mother was going to continue to disapprove, but the night before, she said, 'I don't care, I'm coming to this wedding.'

"This was 1960, when all of the standard hostility was being joined with new black consciousness. My mom just said, 'Look, society's gonna kick your butt if you do this.' And then his family were incredibly opposed to it. They sought advice, went to their minister, talked to their neighbors, and just decided no good could come of this. But on the other hand, they loved their son and over the years we got pretty close, although getting close to his folk is about 1,500 yards away from what I would call close. From the perspective of someone born in a very loving black household, this is pretty cold stuff."

Marriage is not the ideal way to learn about cultural difference, since the contrast between cultures can easily become confused with the contrast between male and female, and any two-way comparison can be interpreted as better and worse, high and low. When I am teaching anthropology, I try to encourage students always to think in terms of three cultures, their own and at least two others—not one other, because they could too easily reduce true human diversity to a single dimension of difference, us and them, civilized and savage. The stereotypes of savages or primitives do not stand up to the awareness of the diverse forms of adaptation of preliterate societies, with their distinctive ingenuities and elaborations. Neither does the stereotype of civilization, which is constantly shifting and revealing an endless series of problems.

If I thought I knew the ideal way of being human, I would teach that instead of the discipline of anthropology.

The Presbyterian mission in Iran that gave birth to Damavand College, where I taught for a while, had the cable address INCULCATE; I guess they thought they knew. Most higher education is devoted to affirming the traditions and origins of an existing elite and transmitting them to new members.

When I think about the real achievements I made at Amherst, it is striking to see how many of them involved a further opening up of the college: opening up through increased interchange with other institutions in the Pioneer Valley that many of my colleagues liked to think of as inferior; opening up the exclusive club of the faculty to other groups; opening up the curriculum to include a broader spectrum of the human experience. The structural and psychological issues of including different groups that have traditionally been excluded are nearly identical. On the one hand, excluded groups need to find ways of affirming their own value, from the search for self-esteem of women in consciousness-raising sessions to the expressions of gay pride, slogans like "black is beautiful," and the struggle to escape from a colonial mentality. On the other hand, the values and potentials of excluded groups need to be made visible and accessible to stimulate the imaginations of those who have always assumed that their way—often the way that benefits them most—is the best.

It was a moment of achievement when the Amherst romance-language department hired, for the first time, not only a native speaker of Spanish but a New-World Hispanic; a moment of achievement when a member of that department undertook to teach French literature originating outside of France. A small college can only teach a limited number of languages, but it can become more inclusive by noticing that French and Spanish, like English, are no longer limited to the Western tradition. The college's temporary soft-money commitment to Japanese was transformed into a permanent department of Asian languages, and we had begun to support a cooperative commitment to Arabic.

Taken together, these were suspect moves, and they made nominal liberals uneasy. My colleagues grumbled about the "camel's nose under the tent," so I bought a small toy camel to stand on my desk, next to the roll of authentic red tape and a wind-up robot labeled FTE (for "full-time equivalent": better than money, FTEs are the ultimate measure of value in terms of budgeted faculty positions). The nose of the camel under the tent is a matter of openness, of lifting up the canvas and making an institution that is preoccupied with the basis of its own privilege open to other kinds of people and other cultural traditions. *Terras irradient,* the Amherst College motto, has tended to be a one-way street.

Because all forms of elitism and exclusion are congruent, the issue of women kept coming up. Sexual, racial, and cultural chauvinism all rest on the same traditional assumptions of dominance based on difference. To be an advocate for the young and insecure could be construed as being an advocate for women. So could any effort away from secrecy and special exceptions toward regular and explicit processes of hiring and promotion, for the old secretive ways supported old patterns of power and privilege. Even a concern for interdisciplinary programs must have seemed like an effort to subvert the god-given disciplinary departments, which provide the traditional power bases of the academy even as they constrict the imagination.

It has been pointed out that all of the world's Universalistic religions originated at the margins of powerful high civilizations. It also seems probable that the most creative thinking occurs at the meeting places of disciplines. At the center of any tradition, it is easy to become blind to alternatives. At the edges, where lines are blurred, it is easier to imagine that the world might be different. Vision sometimes arises from confusion. Women at Amherst were not only outsiders; they also tended to focus their intellectual interest on subjects that were treated as peripheral. Julian Gibbs, who was president when I arrived, defended the need to teach courses on non-Western culture in public. Privately, he confided his conviction that the peoples of Western Europe and the United States must be superior because of their role in the modern development of science.

In 1980, the Amherst political-science department included one woman, an expert on modern China, who was also the only member of the department concerned with nonindustrialized societies. The history department had one woman also, teaching on India, the only untenured member of the department. After she was denied tenure, the department wanted to fill her position with an additional Americanist, but they did agree to seek someone who would teach American women's history, labor history, or minority history. Later, when I queried their selection of a man who was an expert on white male immigrant labor, Julian dismissed the entire original definition of the search. "Loser's history!" he said, "What would they want that for?" and I knew I could not block the appointment. To demonstrate their commitment to diversity, the department asked the man they had chosen to bone up on women.

The certification of privilege has always been as important a function of education as bringing about learning, but there is a possibility that the real winners in a rapidly changing world will be those who are open to alternatives and able to respect and value those who are different. These winners will not require that others become losers. It is not easy for those who start from positions of privilege and are threatened by all change to accept this, but it is also not easy for those who have been outsiders and accepted negative views of their own value. Each of the friends I worked with on this project has been an immigrant learning to live in the new environment of partial equality, and so each of us has had to be open to change, just as our husbands and lovers and colleagues have been challenged to accept new forms of relationship. The change goes on, and surely the central task of education today is not to confirm what is but to equip young men and women to meet that change and to imagine what could be, recognizing the value in what they encounter and steadily working it into their lives and visions.

PARTNERSHIPS

MOST PEOPLE, when asked to describe their life histories, divide them into chapters that are partly conventional, representing stages of maturation, and partly idiosyncratic. Marriage, divorce, and childbearing become chapter headings in women's lives because of the way they produce—or demand—an entire restructuring of life around commitments to others.

When we are fortunate, of course, we have many friends, men and women, and work alongside many different kinds of people, learning and teaching in complex complementarities. But a few relationships become so central that they structure the sense of the whole. To Ellen, the major decision punctuating her life had been the decision to leave academic medicine in order to have a child. I tend to organize my own history around periods of time spent in different countries, as remembered experience with whole communities evokes its context. In the hours we spent together, it was clear that Alice was telling me the story of her life before Jack, with Jack, and after Jack.

Jack died in April 1985. Alice had spent that Saturday at the lab, working on a technical presentation for a conference, and came home to find Jack's body lying on the grass, where he had been cutting brush, already growing cold. Alice telephoned Barkev, Jack's best friend, from the hospital. We joined her, standing in the emergency room, finding the sudden loss so implausible we had nothing to say. Alice cradled the stiff body on the stretcher and said again and again, "I loved him. I loved his body."

"You know," Alice said later, "I didn't cry much in that period of time, I was numb like I wasn't there. I just wanted to die, and then I suddenly saw—you know, you have these revelations—that I was going to die eventually, no problem with that. There was nothing that was going to keep me alive forever, it was just a question of a few years, a very finite period of time. So did I really feel that I couldn't do interesting things in that period of time? That I had to die right then on the spot? I realized that I was in an enormous amount of pain because my life had been so pleasurable, in spite of all the hard things. I used to wake up in the morning beside Jack and look over, and he was very beautiful and childlike, and I would think, how did I become so lucky?

"We always made love in the morning, and it was always lovely, and then we would walk in the woods. He really appreciated all the birds and the geese, and he was interested in everything. It was really a very wonderful life. Because all at once I had what I had always wanted, which was working on the same thing. It meant my head wouldn't be so cluttered with having a work life and then a home life. I have a kind of a simpleminded head that likes everything to be in one direction, all in some sort of a ball."

The story of Alice's life before she met Jack is the story of a search for passionate collaboration, and yet she speaks of the times of intense scientific effort as strangely peaceful, as times of cool lucidity in contrast to the complexity of human emotions. Alice spent six months working with her father on some theoretical aspects of aeronautical engineering to see if she wanted to go back to theoretical research. "He was always a wonderful teacher, but for working together on problems it just didn't work. He expected me to understand everything he did, but I was not allowed to disagree. It's not that he didn't hear what I said, he just sort of dismissed it. And he was giving me very plebian things to do, like reworking French technical reports. I don't know. It's the single thing that has bothered me most about my relations with my father. As a child, I didn't know my mother could think—she was lovely and charming and quick tempered—but my father was really a hero to me. So after that I decided to abandon theoretical work and I joined a computer company." Alice was married at that time to Paul, who was an industrial designer and a colleague. Since then, she has had her most intense relationships with scientists and engineers, men with whom she could share the pleasures of solving technical problems.

Men and women often do their best work in tandem, with a clear sense of common direction and a degree of complementarity that allows not only a division of labor but contrasting approaches to the same problem. Work relationships of any kind are enlivened by difference combined with mutual commitment. Most societies, however, separate the work of men and women when production is no longer based in the family; the tendency is to regard passion or tenderness as distractions. Although we are extraordinarily romantic about marriage, we are curiously blind to the joys and benefits of real partnership. Modern ideas about the relationship between work and home, with a monetary value put on work and a tendency to devalue all forms of labor that do not bring in money, have sharpened this division. What is perhaps more serious is the fact that these separations, like the exclusion of the talents of large sections of the population, have caused us to forego important kinds of creativity. As I talked to my friends about their lives, I was as sharply struck by the diversity of partnerships as by the ingenuity shown in the combination of different kinds of commitments, including the work of homemaking and relationship building, the caring needed to nurture ideas and institutions.

When Jack and Alice met at a party in 1979, Alice was at a point of transition. She was about to leave a job, change apartments, and acknowledge the end of a relationship that had been both romantic and collegial. Jack chimed in on a conversation between Alice and the hostess, who was also an engineer. The conversation moved from engineering careers to gastronomy, both of which fascinated him. Alice found him outrageous and outrageously attractive wearing his ragged jeans, enthusiastically attacking the buffet. They met for lunch and soon became lovers.

Jack was living with his wife, Jean, and their two daughters in Cambridge. The affair with "Lady Alice" appeared to fit into a pattern which Jack told Alice had existed for a long time in his family, describing his household as an open marriage sustained by shared parenthood. When I went to Amherst, Barkev became a long-term weekday bachelor, and on the evenings when Jean worked late, Jack would fix lavish dinners for Barkev and Alice, or the three of them would cook together in his cramped Cambridge house, whose center was clearly the kitchen. The household seemed to settle into an amicable understanding about when Jack would be with his wife and daughters, when Jack would be with Alice, and when everyone would be together with the family and a multitude of other guests coming and going, Sunday-night barbecues in the yard with a butterflied leg of lamb and an extravagant series of different wines.

In December 1981, the equilibrium in another part of Jack's life fell apart. Orion Research, the company he had founded to design and manufacture scientific instruments, had absorbed his and Jean's energies for years. Eventually, Jean became a professional counselor working in the gay community. Jack had remained with Orion, and it became his whole life. It had been successful and had expanded, but in the process Jack had lost majority ownership. There were enough people made uneasy by Jack's iconoclastic style to support an ambitious coup by a vice president, who was able to point to the familiar problems of transition when a company becomes too large to reflect the vision of a single founder. In a sudden move, he and his cohorts presented themselves as acting for the good of the company, and, in the classic mode of coups, ended up occupying the positions of power themselves. Jack was informed that the board of directors no longer wanted him as president.

Jack was devastated as the world he had built up crumbled. "He himself would never destroy anybody," Alice said. "It just never really occurred to him that anyone could undermine him so. Orion meant so much to him. I don't think it ever occurred to him that anyone whom he liked—loved, really—that they could remove the thing that was most important in his life. He was like a wild man, the pain was unbearable to watch. His mind was trying to think of solutions and they were wild, meshuga, because he was in so much pain."

In the weeks that followed, Jack zigzagged between gloom and the manic certainty that he had developed strategies to recover Orion, including an unsuccessful lawsuit. At that point, Alice decided that she could help by getting Jack involved in a new set of technological problems that would channel some of the energy he was putting into plots and counterplots and emotional turmoil. She persuaded him to go with her to various technical conferences and shows and started introducing him to her own area of specialization. Many years earlier a friend had commented to her, "The trouble with computers is not just that they are dumb. They are also blind, deaf, and quadriplegic." Alice's research for the space program and later for a medical-instrument company had zeroed in on questions of the human-machine interface, especially on ways to moderate that blindness, to make it possible to handle more visual information with computers. At the time she and Jack became lovers, she was working at Polaroid and had just completed the initial research on a system for computer-generated slides, eventually marketed under the trademark Palette.

So Alice began to take Jack to trade shows. She was looking from the Polaroid point of view, always involving the transfer of information to film, when Jack suddenly said, "Hah! That's what's missing—the piece of paper. Why can't we get all this very advanced visual material right onto plain paper?" Once Jack had identified a problem they could tackle, they rented space and persuaded a softwear designer to join them, becoming involved in a whole range of copying issues. Jack named the company Demonics, for "on-demand printing by electronics," but it also referred to the printer's devil Jack meant to replace, a multiple pun of the kind that delighted him. It was also a vintage specimen of Jack's deviltry; in the same vein, Jack obtained quarters for the new company right next door to the Orion plant. Demonics started as a way of refocusing Jack's energy; because it depended on both his entrepreneurial vision and Alice's technical knowledge, it soon became a full-scale collaboration.

I was following all this at a distance, as it evolved in a sort of counterpoint to my habitual patterns of relating professional and domestic life. Barkev would arrive each weekend, passing on Jack and Alice's accounts of the drama episode by episode. Both of us were skeptical of their decision to start a company. Later, when Jack moved into Alice's apartment, it seemed to us that they were overloading the relationship and that it would inevitably break down. To me, it echoed the intensity of my parents' relationship, particularly when both of them were doing fieldwork; to Barkev, it went against the pattern he grew up with, which has always sounded to me like a long-term estrangement, lacking intimacy and held together for reasons of conviction. Even when we were first married, we looked with suspicion at couples who lived "in each other's pockets" and did everything together. Our pattern, which involved spending months at a time apart, has nevertheless proved curiously resilient.

Each of the women I talked to has experimented with combinations of work and intimacy. We form a spectrum ranging from mutual support of separate activities to Alice and Jack's compacted layers of involvement. There is a special dynamic in hard creative work alongside someone you are in love with. The ideas flow differently, and there is a common vividness. In heterosexual couples, collaboration is valuable because the woman's goals are not automatically reduced to second rank, even if her contribution often is. A commitment to work shared with a man becomes indistinguishable from commitment to that man, but collaboration may make the woman's contribution invisible, like the nonwork done within the household, or the clerical and managerial work that Jack's wife, Jean, did for years at Orion Research, as deeply invested in those early years as he. Historically, many of the lesbian relationships we know about were between women who gave each other the impetus to enter new careers, opening them up for all women. Women are often stimulated to more ambitious and creative work when they see that work supporting someone they love. In Alice's case, it was clear that she was the more effective of the two as far as technology was concerned, while Jack provided the demonic discontent.

There are many forms of collaboration. To me, Joan Erikson reflects a creative option available to a previous generation. She has always given first priority to the traditional roles of homemaking and childcare, while Erik has always remained rather aloof from them. But she has also contributed directly to his work, working ideas through with him and editing all of his writing. In the interstices, she has taken up projects that are hers alone; these Erik supports and encourages, but again with a certain aloofness. When Joan is working on a book, she reads it aloud to Erik, who applauds but makes little comment. "He's very appreciative and accepting, but he doesn't offer much. It's as if he can't get into my language, or it's a different piece of music from his. But I can get into his language because I've been doing it so long that it's like another voice of mine." When Erik is working on a book, she goes over the text word by word, as she has done since he first started writing in English. Part of her role has been to defend his stylistic idiosyncrasies, insisting that they are part of his voice, not linguistic errors to be corrected and standardized. For me, the working relationship between Joan and Erik evokes memories of the times when I worked with my father.

Johnnetta and her husband Robert began their professional lives in passionate collaboration, falling into love and into political commitment together. After they were married, they went in 1962 to Liberia, where they were to work as members of a research team that was to provide each with dissertation material on the economics of changing patterns of labor from traditional forms to modern industry. This required fieldwork in the villages and within households, so Johnnetta's anthropological work, one day interviewing cab drivers in Monrovia, another day studying household economies in rural areas, made an important contribution to the whole. But more important to Johnnetta's sense of that period as a time of equal contributions and mutual stimulation was the fact that Robert was white and Johnnetta black; being in Africa moved them beyond the asymmetries of black-white relationships in the United States.

"I feel so strongly how important that was for our relationship, because the 'majority culture,' as we say here in Atlanta, looked more like mine in color terms than Robert's, and it was a really important period for solidifying our relationship. Robert was really good in that setting. It was really important to both of us to have someone in an intimate relationship with whom we could work through some of what we were seeing, doing a lightning running analysis, pillow to pillow. We were a dynamite team. Robert is very methodical, so sometimes I wanted to say, Robert, just spit it out; but he works slowly with everything carefully thought out. My mind is much quicker, more erratic, more creative, but the combination was dynamite."

Barkev and I started out thinking of ourselves as having entirely different interests: he was studying mechanical engineering when we met, while I was studying Arabic poetry. But the years we spent in other countries meant that each of us became very much involved in learning the local cultures. I tended to emphasize language and the beliefs and customs of ordinary people, while he was concerned with the relationship between local tradition and industrial and business development, both of us were involved in institution building and feeling the need to communicate effectively with students and colleagues. We have complemented each other in our efforts to understand the environments we have worked in, even though we have seldom actually been colleagues. Today, it is he who reads what I write, chapter by chapter, and presses me to set my sights higher and work at the top of my talent; he makes the invisible contribution that has traditionally been made by women. Some of the dynamic in these relationships comes, as often happens between parent and child, from unrealized dreams. Barkev wonders whether he would have written more without a writer in the house; Joan picks up themes from Erik's youth as an artist.

These collaborative marriages, however productive and satisfying they may be, have to be renegotiated every time there is a move. There are likely to be assumptions about gender built into every new environment and indeed built into the move. Each of the overseas moves that Barkev and I have made together has carried the assumption that my work was an afterthought. He has been the expert imported from overseas; I have been "local hire," picked up because I was available. After working with great satisfaction as equal colleagues in Africa, Johnnetta and Robert returned to the United States in 1962 with a new baby and Robert's mentors helped to arrange a job for him at Washington State University at Pullman. Johnnetta found part-time and temporary jobs in the area, bearing a second child and taking years to complete her dissertation. At Washington, it was clear that Robert's career was primary, and might have remained so except that Johnnetta was playing increasingly conspicuous roles in the emerging activism of the sixties. Eventually she got a regular appointment at Washington State, and in 1970 she was offered a tenured position at the University of Massachusetts and invited to play a key role in developing their Afro-American Studies program. To facilitate the move, the U. Mass. administration undertook to find Robert a temporary position in one of the other institutions in the Five-College Consortium, to give him a chance to find a permanent position. What they found was a visiting professorship in the economics department of Amherst College, but Robert never did find a permanent position in the area. This put him in an increasingly asymmetrical and culturally incongruous situation; when he left Massachusetts to work elsewhere, he abandoned Johnnetta and the marriage as well.

I winced when I heard this story from Johnnetta. I was not at Amherst College at the time, but I knew enough of the attitudes still in existence when I arrived to know that any such arrangement was likely to be doomed. From the point of view of the department he was asked to join, Robert, hired as a spouse, was by definition inferior to Johnnetta, who was inferior to other U. Mass. faculty, and they in turn were inferior to all Amherst faculty. Furthermore, while U. Mass. includes radical ideas within the intellectual range of economics, Robert would have been judged by the Amherst economics department as flatly wrong in his intellectual and social convictions. Robert must have felt a bit as I felt in Iran during the revolution, working along at my job and wondering whether I would lose it more quickly because I was a foreigner, or because I was a non-Muslim, or because I was a woman. Any one of the three would eventually be fatal. Being a woman and black in America generally means one is two strikes down, but the time was right for Johnnetta. Johnnetta's star kept rising, Robert's was repeatedly stalled.

A man and a woman may struggle for equality in their relationship, but external pressures continually destroy the balance. It's not easy to stand together against the world. Society is casually unfair to women, expecting to pay them less and treating their work as intrinsically less valuable than the same job done by a man. But it is often pointedly punitive of men whose decisions do not fit that judgment. One reason that women still accept second-class citizenship is the fear that men who treat them as equals may become pariahs, relegated to well below second class. The academic world is notorious for the nastiness of the power games it plays, sometimes for such very small stakes. But in general, it is every man for himself—unless the issue is one that threatens their common dominance.

In Iran, I had improvised and pieced together a number of different jobs, juggling the extra burdens of childcare and running a household in a strange environment. When we returned to the United States, Barkev urged me to go on the job market without restricting my choices to fit some obvious next step of his. He said that he would accompany me and find a job that would allow us to be together. It turned out that his idea of being together was weekend commuting, which left me running a single-parent household. Still, much as I resented that decision, I feel fortunate that he never moved into a contingent status in the Amherst community.

When a man accepts the vulnerabilities associated with a woman's position, he is doubly vulnerable. For a woman, it is familiar territory.

In the puzzle of composing a life, the interdependence of one's own work with that of someone else is a major complication. Since households must rely more and more on dual incomes, every step must be worked out so that each partner can continue productive work, and both may have to improvise. Men no longer organize their lives around two fully separate narratives, one domestic and one professional; women's narratives are half autonomous and half contingent. Almost any move puts a working couple at risk and reintroduces old inequities, and even commuting is proving less and less workable as the barrier between home and work weakens. The dual-career household may gradually come to inhibit mobility or reduce it to where it was fifty years ago when families were married to land.

When two people work in close tandem, a major change in emphasis by one is likely to affect the whole system. Ellen and her husband Steve, who also practiced as a psychiatrist, started out working in parallel as residents at Beth Israel Hospital, doing very much the same jobs in the same place. After they married, they set out together for the same workplace in the morning and returned together at night, but most of the time they were not working side by side or on the same projects. Ellen was, if anything, slightly senior. They did, however, coauthor a standard reference text on psychoactive medications. The malaise that affected Ellen at thirty-five also affected Steve and led him to move from individual psychotherapy and academic medicine to industrial consulting. He based his new professional life at home, just as Ellen did when she relocated her work to allow for childcare. Parallelism continued. My mother often omitted her first marriage from autobiographical statements because, she said, "we had neither a book nor a baby together." By 1984, Steve and Ellen had both. Writing a book with someone is a curious kind of sharing in the creation of new life, an intimacy that establishes a permanent link even when one moves on to other interests.

In the children's classic, *Mary Poppins,* the father goes to the city every day "to make money," and the children imagine him actually stamping out shillings and pence. This is one end of the pattern, a man disappearing into a world of work that is entirely mysterious to women and children. In an agricultural community, men and women have separate tasks, but these tasks are visibly complementary and familiar to both. In contemporary society, the inclusion of women into more and more fields means that men and women work side by side on parallel tasks. But it also suggests the possibility of new kinds of complementarity.

Alice's strategy of creating a setting in which Jack's involvement with a new technology could flourish—a kind of homemaking—was only partly successful. He continued his ill-fated battles against Orion, including a doomed proxy fight, parking a trailer in front of the Orion door during the annual stockholders' meeting and serving champagne and coffee while he made his case to stockholders. When Jack sued the board of directors, the public fuss ruffled the Boston financial establishment in ways for which he was never forgiven.

Alice and Jack's collaboration also created a new set of problems. After Alice resigned from Polaroid to join Jack in setting up Demonics, the intensity of their work together destabilized the complex equilibrium of Jack's marriage, already battered by months of his shifting moods of anger and depression. His wife announced, after a brief period of marriage counseling, that she had had enough.

So Jack showed up one Saturday morning with six shopping bags and his Labrador retriever at the door of Alice's condominium in Boston's Italian North End, a section of a renovated loft with a high living room, a partially partitioned kitchen area, and a single bedroom—Jack, who occupied the space of five people with his bursts of enthusiasm and vehemence, his waving arms, and his desire to prepare feasts for multitudes. Alice suddenly found that her love affair had mushroomed into every corner of her life. Meantime, she was carrying the main R&D load at work, desperately trying to develop a product before the money ran out.

For her birthday, Jack bought Alice a television, "because I didn't have one and he liked to watch TV, and I cried. All at once he was moving in, and he was going to change my life and fill it up with noise and clutter from other people, and I was just kind of the maid. So the next thing is, I do a big birthday party for his two girls and I work real hard—I'm always obsessed when I'm doing food—and I'm really stressed out at work and tired and no one is helping. So I go into the bedroom and put on walking shoes and leave. I walk for a couple of hours and cool down, and when I come back there's nobody there but Jack. He's washing the dishes and he's looking so hurt that I can't stand it and I immediately start to cry. I say, I was just trying to make myself feel good, not to hurt you, and he's just so hurt, so cute."

After that, Jack went househunting, selling his Orion stock at the top of its market value. He had maintained a paradoxical image of penury and extravagance during all the years we had known him; now, he bought a palatial estate in Dover, called Riverbend because the Charles River curved gracefully across the bottom of its broad landscaped lawns. There was a small formal garden with a cast-iron statue of a rooster, two wild Canadian geese that lived at the river's edge and came to the kitchen door for handouts every morning, and an extensive stable that became the home for the pair of peacocks that Jean gave him as a housewarming present. Above all, there were enough rooms for solitude. When Alice moved in with her harpsichord she also kept her North End apartment as a pied-à-terre where they could stay after working late in the city and a place she could retreat to by herself.

Then began the siege—a desperate effort to build Demonics into a viable enterprise, while Jack's money seemed to melt away on salaries and equipment. It was a race against time to develop the technology, with Jack peering over everyone's shoulder and asking questions that reopened basic assumptions. The venture capitalists came and went, deciding one after the other that the whole project was too risky for them: Jack was seen as too much of a maverick, Alice's role was too ambiguous. During this period, one venture capitalist explained to Alice that given the Orion history, Jack would never get financing in Boston. (After Jack's death, when Alice became CEO, another venture capitalist was kind enough to explain to Alice that the company would never get financing under her leadership because she was a woman.) When Jack had put in two million dollars from the sale of his Orion stock and the money was almost gone, the staff of the company, now consisting of a dozen people, took across-the-board salary cuts. The most ominous fact was that Jack had poured in the money from the sale of the Orion stock without having paid capital-gains taxes.

The break barely came in time. A Japanese company, Canon, recognized the complementarity between the Demonics technology and their new-generation copiers. They moved toward a multilayered relationship that would begin with a preliminary technology-transfer contract, with Demonics working on a set of Canon's technical problems. Jack went on a negotiating trip to Japan in February 1985 and on a second one in April. He came back knowing they had won a breathing space and he would not go to jail for his unpaid taxes, and prepared a celebratory dinner of mussels and grilled salmon and fine wine with Alice and Barkev. The next afternoon, Jack died.

During his battle for professional survival, Jack had put off the details of divorce and remarriage and writing a new will, so he left Alice neither an heir nor a widow. She moved quickly out of Riverbend, taking nothing except what was indisputably her property: her personal possessions, her harpsichord, and a stray dog that had adopted her and Jack. Jack's portrait went up on the wall of her North End condo and his pillow, with a lingering scent of his presence, stayed in her bed. When she woke in the despairing hours long before dawn, she would dress quickly and take Cheska, the big dog, for swift ferocious walks through the darkness.

But Alice was more than a woman who had lost her lover and her home, with no public standing from which to grieve. She was still married to the effort of those long months and still the person who had given form to Demonics, her technical knowledge and concern for an effective working team supporting Jack's flashes of erratic brilliance. More and more, she lived at the office. Over the next year, her commitment to Jack evolved into a commitment to guide the still-struggling company, renamed Rise Technology, through the next stages of its life. Her impulse to help Jack deal with his losses through creativity changed slowly into a thoughtful questioning of the kind of leadership that would make the company a place where many creative people could do their best work.

GIVE AND TAKE

PART OF THE SECRET of continuing development—
especially for women, who may be pressed by social expectations into childlike positions of weakness—is the discovery
through a variety of relationships that social expectations can
be changed and that difference can be a source of strength
rather than of weakness. We grow in dialogue, not only in the
rare intensity of passionate collaboration, but through a multiplicity of forms of friendship and collegiality.

Throughout this project, I have been pursuing questions of friendship and collegiality. Each of the five of us
seems to seek out relationships across difference, and yet we
are all sensitive to the treatment of difference as invidious
that is so common in American culture. Joan, for instance,

has done much of her work in the highly hierarchical and degree-conscious world of the mental hospital, and she speaks with forgiving frustration of the slowness of doctors to recognize the complementary contributions of others to treatment, to recognize that the work artists do with patients could be as essential as that of physicians.

"They don't think anybody has anything unless they can put it into language. I said, art is a language, and it's too bad that you don't understand it. I couldn't believe my ears. The Activities Program is absolutely sacrosanct now in its own little building at Riggs, and I don't think anyone would touch it. They know they get patients because of it. But what baffles me is that although all this is true, you cannot get the doctors to think through what is happening there. They still want to be the successful ones—to say that it was the therapy that did it. Even though you can show that the turning point has come, say, working on a painting. I don't know what's going on with these MDs, but they can't bring themselves to think seriously about it theoretically. They'll say, yes, it's important, and we wouldn't be without it: but it just seems too hard for them to say that their work isn't what's doing it, because they work very hard and they care very much. I really believe that. I think it's the combination of the two things that changes people, the Activities Program *and* the therapy. But it's very hard to do what the Activities people do and get so little credit.

"The doctors have stopped using certain kinds of language, though. It's subtle but it's made a mark. They don't take on the stance of the therapist any more and just say, look what *I* did. So obviously, the nurses have contributed and the

Activities Program too. They have some woman therapists now, and they are much more careful, and the men are learning from them. It pleased me. I spent my whole time, when I was in emergency recently, watching my doctor, who was a woman, and the other women, and seeing that the men treated them with real respect. When the women speak to you you feel like a person, and when the men speak to you, you feel like a patient, but they're learning different. I enjoyed this. But I don't think there's anything you can do but muddle along the way we're doing, writing about it and trying to get men off the high horse where they have so little air—they're up so high there's not enough ozone, they're really not feeling and sensing what they should about the world. It's not enviable." Joan laughed and told me a story about Erik being challenged on something he wrote about "penis envy" years ago. "Did I write that?" he said. "Well, I was wrong."

While we seem to seek interdependence and respect across difference, the best possibility offered by our culture seems to be the hope of equality. Johnnetta and I compared notes on our experiences in academic administration. Both of us were sometimes handicapped and sometimes helped by complementarities. She worked as associate provost at the University of Massachusetts under a provost named Loren Baritz. "That man and I really hit it off. I was not afraid of Loren like most people, so I served as a very valued member of his staff. People in high positions are often surrounded by loyalty and hypocrisy, people who tell you you're great, but we had a straightforward honest relationship built on mutual respect." I commented that there was another side to this.

Julian Gibbs, college president during my time at Amherst, simply could not tolerate disagreement from a male in his age range. He would react to the symmetry of the relationship and go immediately into an adversarial mode, like a fighting cock. He depended on me because his need to play rivalrous male games made discussion and criticism nearly unavailable to him, except from women.

"Not just a woman, in my case," Johnnetta said, "a black woman. I say that because Loren had a very similar relation with Esther Terry, one of my closest friends. The three of us were quite a team. Loren Baritz never ever patted me on the head, and I never saw him figuratively pat Esther on the head. I would literally have walked out of that office the first day he did. This man just did not treat us in a paternalistic or a racist manner. We were on his case, and he could take it because we were black women, but he didn't need to put us down to bolster his ego.

"My problem at U. Mass. wasn't Loren Baritz, it was lots of men with extremely tweeded minds. I tell you—well, I don't have to tell *you*—there are some very insecure white males in the academy who are deeply threatened by anybody that looks and sounds like me. Or you. Somebody that's smart and male and white is bad enough, but you should come around with that in the other gender and my God the other color! When Loren Baritz asked me to head up a process of curriculum reform, he knew quite well that he was putting me up for the task that is surely the most threatening in the academic world, because it fundamentally questions the value of what people are doing. To ask faculty to change a curriculum is like asking someone to move a graveyard. It can be done but it is a funky, messy, complicated, long process. That was my main task—to lead that faculty through education reform, something in which I did not succeed, if by that is meant that the faculty voted for the general education program I led them in creating. That faculty basically said, hell no. I think they were voting on several things, how they felt about Loren Baritz, how they felt about Johnnetta Cole, and how they felt about themselves. Eventually the faculty passed something that is just mush. If I had gone through the general education vote five years earlier, I think I would have been absolutely crushed by it all. But by that time I think I had a pretty fair understanding of how things work in the academy. Some of that stuff was incredibly nasty, with all the things you know about and went through at Amherst—distinguished colleagues grinning in your face and going behind your back and stabbing the hell out of you. All of which is OK if they wouldn't be so self-righteous, if they wouldn't keep separating themselves from the corporate world, from those *nasty* people in business!"

Talking with Johnnetta made me think back over a series of my own collaborations. One of the most productive was with Dick Goldsby, an immunologist with whom I coauthored a book, *Thinking AIDS*. I met him at Amherst, but he was far from being one of the old boys there, for he was already a respected researcher when he was recruited to fill a professorship endowed specifically for a distinguished black scientist. Shortly after I left Amherst, he moved to the University of Massachusetts to find a better research environment. Our work on AIDS started with my asking him questions about the medical aspects of the epidemic while he pressed me on its meaning to a social scientist. Four years and many questions later, Dick telephoned and suggested that we write a book together. I sent him the draft of an essay I had just written about AIDS and minorities. Six months later, we went to press.

I had left western Massachusetts by the time we started, so it was a commuting collaboration, and our spouses did not even have the possibility of commiserating with each other while we worked. Most of the work was done in Amherst, while Dick's wife, the biologist Barbara Osborne, went back and forth to her lab at U. Mass. and Barkev fended for himself in Cambridge. We would work intensely for a week and then go back to normal life for three weeks or a month, reading and talking and letting the new chapters settle until we could coordinate another week together. In the evenings, Dick and Barbara and I talked biology over the dinner table. I probably learned more and better biology because Barbara was there, for she often rejected simplifications and slipped into fully professional discussions with Dick, while I pulled them back to my level when things became excessively technical. Dick and Barbara have parallel but asynchronous careers, with common interests and techniques but over a decade's difference in trajectory.

Dick and I worked well together because our interests interlocked. He did not assert or defend dominance, either as a male or as a natural scientist; nor was he troubled by the fact that he had known me first as a dean. Each of us had knowledge and skills the other lacked; we had no need to prove that one set of skills was superior to the other or to conceal our areas of ignorance. Our rhythms were sufficiently different to stimulate each of us to work harder: I was often up making coffee an hour or two before Dick and Barbara, throwing myself at a new chapter with a dozen pages of draft by noon, burnt out by two or three. Dick was inclined to offer me serious books to read when I wanted to bury my nose in the oblivion of a detective story, but Barbara had a supply to draw on. As a team, Dick and I were equal but profoundly complementary. We had the genuine differences that allowed each of us to meet a need in the other, pursuing mysteries that only the other could unravel, with a delight in mutual teaching and learning. The man had things in his head I wanted to know, and my ideas fell into place when he asked critical questions. We worked toward clarity as he chided me for too much idealism and I coaxed him away from the traditional military metaphors for the immune system, drawing my own imagery from ecology rather than warfare.

For complementarity to be truly creative, it is not sufficient for need to run in both directions; it is necessary to acknowledge that both contributions are of equal value and that both are freely given. This is fundamentally different from the way people in America thought about male-female relationships when I was growing up. Even today, the labor of women in the home, because it is unpaid, is often not acknowledged as genuinely necessary and valuable work. Because women have lacked alternatives, their work has not had the value of that which is freely chosen. The inequality established in this way and supported by the culture at large has worked as a sort of underlying premise of the male-female relationship and of other relationships as well. Such inequality depends on cultivated blindness; it is reinforced by convergent evidence and unaffected by contradiction.

In fact, this is only one way we are limited in our thinking about the give and take of diverse relationships. For a long time, I was puzzled about how to think about my relationship with the women who worked with me on this book. This is a multiple collaboration built on both difference and similarity, but I still lack an appropriate term for it. Before and beyond this project, we are clearly friends, but the word is too rich and broad to focus the special commonality of a single project. Sometimes I refer to Joan, Ellen, Johnnetta, and Alice as "the women I have been working with"—as collaborators—and yet this belies the playfulness of many of our conversations. The words used by social scientists for those they involve in their research feel wrong to me, even though as an anthropologist I believe that the people we call "informants" are our truest colleagues. These women are not "interviewees," not "subjects" in an experiment, not "respondents" to a questionnaire. There is symmetry in our mutual recognition but there is asymmetry in that I am the one who goes off and weaves our separate skeins of memory into a single fabric. But they weave me into their different projects, too.

The usual words fit even less well when I apply them to myself as the fifth member of the group, to me interviewing myself, asymmetry within symmetry. Women have been particularly interested in the notion of reflexivity, of looking inward as well as outward. Perhaps this is because we are not caught in the idea that every inspection involves an inspector and an inspectee, one inevitably dominant, the other vulnerable.

When I search for a word for my relationship with the women described in this book, I feel a need for a term that would assert both collegiality and the fact that the process is made possible by our differences. The thesaurus betrays me, denying me a term that affirms both symmetry and complementarity. The gap in the language parallels a gap in the culture. We are rich in words that describe symmetrical relationships, from buddy to rival to colleague. We are also rich in words that describe strongly asymmetrical relationships, many of which imply hierarchy and have curious undertones of exploitation or dominance. But none of the words meets my needs.

This puzzlement that afflicts me is compounded when I ask these four women about their other relationships. All have many dimensions of difference, never steadily symmetrical, even though we may describe them with symmetrical language. Johnnetta laughed when I pressed her to describe the men and women she felt closest to in her years of research in Cuba, people who were surely both friends and informants. "This sounds like grade school," she said, "everyone saying, who's your 'ABC'—who's your 'ace boon coon'?" But then she talked me through a rich network of relationships, some of them going back more than a decade to her first trip to Cuba, with artists and doctors and party officials, men and women—relationships of mutual discovery too different to rank in the grade school manner and indeed so different as to almost need separate words for each. These relationships are difficult to sort in other ways, too; people who at one moment acted as guides, at another as students. We are all aware of the importance of mentoring today, but the line between mentor and friend is evanescent. Friends guide and learn from each other, especially in unexplored terrain.

Many years ago, I heard a sermon preached by a Tibetan Buddhist abbot, Nechung Rinpoche. This sermon comes back to haunt my thinking about human relationships and indeed coaxes me beyond human relationships to a vision of relationships throughout the living world. His sermon was a traditional meditation, he explained, developed to lead toward compassion for all sentient beings. He pointed out that we are all—humans, birds, insects, mammals—passing through multiple reincarnations, in and out of these various forms, and we have been doing this throughout eternity. Because time is infinite, so too is the number of reincarnations, so that all possible combinations must have occurred. It follows that I can contemplate any other sentient being— the dog sleeping on the rug by my feet who sighs deeply from time to time, the bird that hunts small insects across the window pane and taps and flutters against it again and again, the wasp caught in the screen, the next person to ring my telephone—and reflect that somewhere in that infinity of time, in some unknown form, this other being was my mother. And from this recognition, the monk said, it is possible to arrive at compassion for all sentient beings.

The monk was a small man, standing in his orange robes and wrinkled by many years of age and exile. He paused at that point, looking a little weary, and said, "You know, I don't find that my American students always feel that way about their mothers. So I advise them instead to meditate on the recognition of the best friend."

The monk was right at two levels about Americans. American men are firmly encouraged to move away from closeness to their mothers, with really strong ties considered slightly pathological, not quite manly. This is part of an emphasis on emotional separation and autonomy that may hamper certain kinds of intimacy—or even compassion—for many men throughout their lives. At a more abstract level, the monk recognized that the ethical impulse of American culture is toward symmetry. When we call it equality, it is both our best and our worst passion, as central to our ethical understanding as the impulse of compassion is to a Buddhist. When we call it competition, we are asserting that it is the fundamental mechanism of the biological world and the well-spring of economics.

Nothing in our tradition gives interdependence a value comparable to symmetry. It is difference that makes interdependence possible, but we have difficulty valuing it because of the speed with which we turn it into inequality. This means that all of the relationships in which two people complement each other—complete each other, as their differences move them toward a shared wholeness—man and woman, artist and physician, builder and dreamer—are suspected of unfairness unless they can be reshaped into symmetrical collegiality. But symmetrical relationships and exchanges alone are limiting. I can think of my warm-blooded and furry dog as a companion (although if I overdo it I will miss much that is fascinating about her), but similarity is less helpful in making me understand the bird and the wasp. Similarity is certainly a premise of this book—but the interest comes from the differences in our situations and stories.

A single dimension of difference is not enough. If two alternatives are contrasted in only one way, they may seem easily ranked, as grade-school children rank their buddies. If the differences multiply, ranking is harder. If the farmer decides whether to plant cotton or corn on the basis of cash value per acre, his decision may seem simple, but he will end up with a single crop, vulnerable to pests and blights and gluts on the market. If he considers many different factors in making his decision, including long-term resilience and soil maintenance, he will probably rotate and diversify. If one attends to multiple dimensions, superiority becomes as elusive as simple equality.

To different degrees, each of the five of us has been discriminated against because we are women; we have all sometimes been treated as less than equal. But each of us seeks out relationships of difference, a little puzzled by the necessary political thrust toward equality. Unless we treasure our differences, we will never achieve interdependence.

The American ethical response to discrimination is the passion for equality, for asserting that a given kind of difference is, or should be, irrelevant and that the task of social justice is to construct a society that will make it so. Thus, social justice is achieved by installing the moral equivalent of wheelchair ramps to provide the appearance of equal access. In general, we seem to believe that the way to achieve fairness is to structure social conflicts so they will be as nearly symmetrical as possible; we then encourage competition between rivals on what is meant to be a level playing field. As a society, we do not believe that outcomes can be expected to be equal, but we do like to believe that it could have gone either way. When the big guy beats the little guy, we like to see him do it with one hand tied behind his back.

This love for symmetry entails a preference for adversarial processes, whose symmetry is often illusory. Take a multimillion-dollar corporation in conflict with a private citizen. Set up a courtroom confrontation, *Megacorp* v. *Doe,* each represented by counsel, with symmetrical rules of play. Sometimes indeed Doe does win, but Doe may grow old and Megacorp grow richer before anything is resolved. The legal fiction that corporations are persons is a way of creating the illusion of symmetry. The doctrine of "one person, one vote" similarly creates the illusion that every citizen has an equal voice in choosing representatives and therefore in determining policy.

It is often the case, as exemplified in the Buddhist meditation, that ethical systems are built on familial metaphors. The American system is based on the metaphor of an idealized relationship between brothers, potential equals for whom affection is mixed with competition. Although they will probably set out in different directions, brothers still should have a comparable chance in life. But brothers have rarely been truly equal, and sisters even less so, especially in societies based on a patrimony, like land, that cannot be divided as easily as a flock of sheep.

In fact, the human experience of relationship starts from a profound asymmetry—the asymmetry between the very small child and the adults on whom he or she totally depends. Yet even this relationship is not as unequal as it appears. Although children are small and physically helpless, their capacity for rapid learning and problem solving is impressive—it is just that the adult carries around a fund of learned solutions. Children might be better off if parents were more aware of themselves as learning from them, rejuvenated by them, and ultimately perhaps dependent on them. The experience of symmetrical relationships with peers and siblings is normally learned later, and yet it is this secondary comradeship with peers that we have valued as an ethical model, especially for men.

When any relationship is characterized by difference, particularly a disparity in power, there remains a tendency to model it on the parent-child relationship. Even protectiveness and benevolence toward the poor, toward minorities, and especially toward women have involved equating them with children. Within this algebra of comparison, women are like children—and women are most likely to be protected and valued when the equation holds, when they are younger and vulnerable. Most men seem to be relatively comfortable with women in subordinate or junior positions, so pretty young coeds are more acceptable than mature women executives. Even when organizations become integrated, there is still the phenomenon called the glass ceiling: women rise as long as there is a layer of more powerful men above them, whose sense of appropriate relationships is not threatened by the women's aspirations. Men may indeed appear to be supporters of women while still holding tightly to superiority.

I knew a senior college professor who, when his institution started to appoint women to the faculty, acquired the reputation of being especially supportive of women by offering to share his office with first one young woman colleague and then another. He repeated this gesture four or five times (the attrition rate for women was notably high), even offering to share his library study with a young woman in another department. Although private offices were standard in the institution, the women were expected to be grateful. When the department finally appointed a woman to a senior position, she too was asked to share, because this curious hands-off variant of droit du seigneur had become a department tradition. "This poor child," he called a woman in her thirties in a tenure discussion. Kindness like this, which is premised on dominance, is doubtfully preferable to simple misogyny. The misogynist works to exclude women; the friendly father figure works to keep them infantile. As women mature and acquire a certain authority based on experience, they encounter increasing resistance and forfeit the illusory good will that goes with being young and respectful. Sexism slides into a version of agism.

Tokenism works in a similar way. Just as a few women with limited authority may be admitted to all-male communities, the presence of one or two lone women as the youngest members of a governing committee provides an analogous form of dependency. Women of my generation have experienced the still-incomplete transition from a period of token integration, when a tiny number of women were admitted to the club, to a period when women are asking for full participation. Suddenly, there is a sharp change in the relatively benevolent attitudes of those willing to tolerate, even be elaborately kind to, a few women in marginal positions.

Women in our society are encouraged to explore complementary relationships, to both trust and nurture. They are permitted to remain closer to their mothers than men and are given primary responsibility for rearing children. Traditionally, women expected inequality in marriage, looking for husbands who were older, taller, richer, and more intelligent than themselves. Not surprisingly, these same husbands continue to earn more and expect their careers to take precedence. We used to be taught to avoid even the appearance of equality lest it threaten the marriage and lead to competition and conflict. Today, women seek equality, but the male game of "Anything you can do, I can do better" makes for a dull world. The most important reason for valuing differences is that they are productive of creativity.

Over a four-year period after Jack's death, Alice was involved in business negotiations with Canon on behalf of Demonics, renamed Rise Technology. I was concerned when I first heard this, because I think of Japan, especially Japanese business, as a very difficult setting for a woman. But for Alice, it worked well. Instead of trying to function like a man, and instead of trying to persuade the Japanese to deal in the same way as Americans, as equals potentially in competition, Alice immersed herself in Japanese styles and went out of her way to emphasize the potential complementarity in the relationship. The first step was composing a long letter after Jack's death, describing the situation and hopes of the company, as she prepared to step into his role in the negotiations. She very deliberately chose a woman to translate her letter into Japanese and to write it in elegant and feminine calligraphy. The reply was a letter advancing the date for the transfer of the half million dollars already agreed on with Jack and an invitation for Alice to go to Japan.

"I explained my ideas there, and why we think we can work synergistically with Canon so the two businesses won't compete. Finally there's a meeting with the top boss, and then we're invited to dinner that night. They didn't want us to go to venture capitalists, so they had asked me how much we needed, and I came up with $3.6 million, and we agreed in general principle on how much they would want as stock, and how it would be spread over time. So then we go off to dinner and there's a lot of sake and we go into the barroom and sing. I'm supposed to sing 'Tennessee Waltz,' and then I join in a Japanese duet written out for me in roman letters, and one of them sings 'Love Me Tender,' which Jack had sung when he was there, and I cried. They're very warm, and we dance in a group with the Mamasan, and it's really warm and loving and nice and I fall asleep and have a headache the next day. But I got the draft agreement we had talked about."

I asked Alice whether being a woman complicated her task. "Well," she said, "one of them did say he didn't want to negotiate with me because he liked women and that made it too tough—that was the only reference to my being a woman. We have wonderful repartee. What I think is that my situation allowed me to behave in a way that feminine characteristics did not impede toughness. The business was easy to do just because of the toughness of the situation. We held the line but we worked on their time scale. And when we agreed to something, we honored it. But they also said not only could I work, but I also knew how to play. I continued to write letters in Japanese when appropriate, and I staged meetings like Nō plays, very dramatic, where I played a civilized part, and we sent each other cards with very carefully chosen haiku. Everything is very individualized because I now know the people and I know what to say. Indeed, now I have people whom I visit, and I get invited very regularly to people's houses."

The relationship between tiny Rise Technology and Canon was inevitably lopsided, but it was built on respect. Rise was able to contribute a technique for reproducing grays and shading that Canon needed, and Canon was able to offer needed schematics to Rise and provide protection for their patents, in addition to giving them desperately needed capital. But what was even more important was that Rise had a different and more flexible style of approaching problems that Canon wanted their engineers to learn, so they started sending engineers for internships in Cambridge. "The coup was finding the right partner, powerful enough to enforce the patents. We wanted their part of the technology, but we could add to it from our knowledge because they weren't doing such a good job. They were concerned that we would begin to compete. Well, you know, you can always compete about anything, but you can always set things up so a small company can do things a large company doesn't want. We wanted to compete in a world that's very niched and no one cares much about it because it's only $50 or $100 million and they're looking for the billion."

The creative possibilities of complementarity were underlined for Joan and me in 1966 when we both sat in on a seminar Erik was leading on history and the life cycle. I was doing a project on Saint Teresa of Avila and reading Saint John of the Cross. They made an interesting pair because each led a reform in his or her branch of the Carmelite order, and each supported the other in what they saw as a single search for union with the divine. Yet there were deep differences in their assumptions. There have been a number of couples like this in religious history, men and women who saw themselves as united in the same ardent search and supported each other in a single historical task, yet who had complementary ways of working. Joan and I started talking about using such pairs to study the differences between men's and women's forms of religious expression, and Joan undertook to write about Saint Francis of Assisi in relation to Saint Clare, the woman around whom he established a women's order similar to the Franciscans in its commitment to poverty, but enclosed in convents while the male Franciscans became mendicant friars scattered across the countryside. Francis and Clare perfectly exemplified much of what Erik was saying in those days about gender differences in relation to inner and outer space. Teresa and John developed a different complementarity; both contemplative, John was the more intensely introspective, while Teresa proved to be an effective organizer and institution builder. As I read the writings of the Carmelite saints, I could see a certain echo of the complementarity between my parents.

Joan wrote up her research in a book called *Saint Francis and His Four Ladies,* which marked the beginning of her interest in the relationship between the role of real women, like Saint Clare, and symbolic women, like the Lady Poverty. I presented my research in the seminar but never published it, for that spring my husband and I packed up and left for the Philippines. As Joan and I talked and compared notes, it became clear that although complementarity was a central ingredient in the kind of creativity we were looking at, important enough to override the strong bias of the age, there was more than one way to develop it.

During the late sixties and early seventies, many women changed their ways of thinking about themselves by joining consciousness-raising groups. Here, women gave one another mutual support and pooled their experiences, adding an analytical process of mutual comparison to move toward insight. At its best, this technique tolerates and values differences, but for many women, the greatest discovery of these groups was that other women could be companions rather than rivals. They learned the value of shared experiences and the benefits of solidarity, becoming friends. In the years since, cooperative and egalitarian relationships—ordinary friendships—have become increasingly important between women and men as well.

Consciousness raising was significant for approximately a decade. By the end of that time, although many problems remained unsolved, large numbers of women embodied the new ways of thinking, which had also been institutionalized in organizations and built into the training of great numbers of professionals. As the sense of discovery was reduced, such groups inevitably became less exciting. Today, members of that generation are often concerned that younger women take their options for granted and, more seriously, that they have lost the vision of what full participation by women might bring to society.

I participated in a consciousness-raising group for about a year during the early seventies. Although I learned a great deal, it was an uncomfortable experience because, as the oldest member of the group, I had coped too well for too many years with the multiple demands of my different roles not to be suspected of being that unpopular creature, the "superwoman," who makes life difficult for other women by bearing burdens that no one should be asked to bear. And I was insufficiently angry. It was not until I had been an object of discrimination myself and been frustrated in my efforts as a dean to achieve fairness for the sake of others that I became angry. Working on this project has been a form of consciousness raising for me, carrying me beyond the discovery of anger; the interwoven stories of these different women may provide something of the same experience for others.

Today, I believe that we will not learn to live responsibly on this planet without basic changes in the ways we organize human relationships, particularly inside the family, for family life provides the metaphors with which we think about broader ethical relations. We need to sustain creativity with a new and richer sense of complementarity and interdependence, and we need to draw on images of collaborative caring by both men and women as a model of responsibility. We must free these images from the connotations of servitude by making and keeping them truly elective.

Increasing numbers of women work now within the symmetrical model, because the asymmetries of gender relationships have been so profoundly exploitative and the discovery of comradeship so rewarding. But symmetrical models promote competition and conflict; as the Bible shows, brothers are not always friends. These models also involve pressing participants toward similarity, teaching them to play by the same rules and to abandon their different styles and different contributions. The loss is serious. Furthermore, symmetrical models work badly across cultures, when differences are real and profound. They are almost useless as a basis for forming ethical relationships outside the human species; they don't help us deal responsibly with the rain forests or the oceans.

The sermon by the Tibetan monk evokes compassion with a double twist: On the one hand, it invites acknowledgment of similarity, reminding the listener that all sentient beings are caught in the cycle of incarnations and have passed through the same forms. We are all alike. On the other hand, it evokes the asymmetry of the mother-infant relationship, of love and mutual need based on difference. We need the rain forests and the living oceans to sustain our lives. Compassion is a more complex idea than equality, but the very word is distorted in Western usage into something like the faintly scornful pity felt by the strong for the weak. "Interdependence" is the word increasingly used for relationships of interlocking needs that contain elements of difference and elements of commonality. We speak of interdependence between species, between nations, between north and south, between different bioregions. Oddly, as procreation becomes less central, we are finding ourselves in need of new ways to express the interdependence of males and females as partners or as friends.

When you hear someone describing their day-to-day interactions, you can sort out the underlying metaphors, listening for the formal similarities between different forms of caring, or rivalry, or exploitation. You find teachers who are aware of learning from their students and teachers who are not; employers for whom workers are interchangeable and others who recognize that spontaneity and freedom produce higher productivity than adversarial negotiations about standardized tasks. Even in working with computers, there is a variation between those who use an imagery of collaboration and those who think in terms of a master-slave relationship. "I always like the aspect where there is a close human interface," Alice commented, "those things a machine can do better because a human being and a machine work together."

The differences between men and women are our most important resource in learning new ways of thinking about difference. We cannot change the disparity between infant and adult, though we can surely learn to understand and respect children more. But we can work toward households and schools in which the differences between men and women are visibly a mutual source of strength rather than dominance. A home is one model of the kind of complex whole two people—or more—can work together to create. This dimension of homemaking is also applicable to the building of laboratories and the staffing of offices, to making places where adults as well as children can grow, where strengths are fostered and possibilities are increased.

Women have a great deal to offer to this process today, but not because they necessarily bring the resources of nurturance and tolerance that create reform. Rather, having grown up expecting to be homemakers and caretakers, they still retain an understanding of interdependence. If they continue looking for complementary relationships, relationships of mutual give and take, when they have rejected inferior status, they can help to make these relationships more widely available. And when women argue against the various forms taken by the exploitation of women, against the premises on which traditional gender relationships and visions of the life cycle have been built, they are also arguing against the arrogant dominance and casual exploitation of the planet on which we live.

If the difference between male and female can be affirmed without connotations of inferiority and superiority, we may be able to change the exploitative elements in other relationships across differences like race and class and, more profoundly, between the developed world and the developing world, between the human species and the rest of the biosphere.

MAKING
AND KEEPING

You keep a house, but you make a home. The word "home" has many layers of meaning. The distinction in English between house and home, even though it is abused by real-estate brokers, is one of our great riches.

The five women in this book have all been homemakers, but none of us keeps house in order to define who we are. Still, we have all been responsible for seeing that, one way or another, the chores got done, though not necessarily promptly or well. As I have puzzled over the ways in which men and women compose their lives, I have come to think of homes as joint compositions, frameworks of complementarity composed by difference within which growth is possible. This concept can be expanded to include schools and neighborhoods, the workplace and the biosphere. Once we accept this redefinition, we can turn the metaphor around and look afresh at our ideas of family residences for rest and work and play. We are creating and sustaining our homes in new ways, forging new links between the abstraction of "home" and its material tokens. As we free the ideas of home and homemaking from their links to old gender roles, we can now also draw on metaphors of home to enrich our perceptions of the world.

Ellen and Steve bought their house in Chestnut Hill, outside of Boston, before the explosion of real-estate prices and interest rates. It's a big old house that allows them to put up players who come to town for tournaments at the nearby Longwood Tennis Club, and could not contrast more sharply with the poverty and homelessness Ellen deals with every day. It seems to cry out for a tribe, and Ellen and Steve, who both grew up in big families, have kept it populated with family on long visits, friends, students, and large golden retrievers. In effect, their impulses have repeatedly moved them away from the image of home as a private base from which to go out. Instead, this is home as an incubator, a place where growth is fostered and relationships reaffirmed. The work involved is shared, while both of them go out to professional activity that involves caring for others, fostering relationships, and promoting growth.

The homes we create for ourselves are far more than physical shelters; the homeless lack far more than homes. In her efforts to improve the care of the homeless, Ellen emphasizes that being homeless means a breakdown of social ties and supports of all kinds. Rooms and apartments are desperately needed not only because they provide shelter but because they foster human relationships within and around them. Those who lack the skills to sustain such relationships need a whole range of supports, including mental and physical health care.

When Ellen and Steve were residents, they shared an apartment without any clear commitment. Getting their first dog, Rusty, established their partnership as a long-term relationship and the space they lived in as a home. The dogs they have today, Obie and Suzie, are both demanding. Obie is a pushy old man who paws insistently or shoves his graying muzzle onto your lap; Suzie is an insecure and needy young female who was kept alone in an outdoor kennel for the first few years of her life and has never completely learned to trust the good fortune that brought her into warmth and companionship. Obie can be shut in the kitchen or the yard when his demands become exasperating, but Suzie stays with Ellen all day when she is working at home, clinging to the comfort of her presence and refusing to eat when she is away.

The household is a choreography of large and small mammals, pursuing their own cross-purposes. Steve and Ellen have experimented with different kinds of childcare workers, incorporating them into family life, but even so they find themselves recruiting every eight months or so, building a new set of rhythms, even as their children are growing and exploring. Danny, the oldest, is bright-eyed and exploratory, demanding attention as he assembles and disassembles his toys, while Sarah has been a calm and smiling baby. Throughout it all, golden retrievers flow across the human current, nudging and leaning. Steve does most of the cooking in this family, and there are also regular trips for Chinese and gourmet take-out. The impulse to domesticity expressed by this large warm house has somehow escaped the temptation of perennial elaborate meals. There is an elegant dining room with grass-papered walls, tall draped windows, and a table that can seat a dozen people, but as often as not, the table is set with cardboard containers of seafood and pasta salads and plastic soda bottles.

When Johnnetta came to Spelman, she came to live alone in Reynolds Cottage, for none of her three sons expect to live here. The youngest, Che, was still in high school, and he stayed on in Johnnetta's New York apartment with his older brother David to finish his senior year.

Reynolds Cottage bears the scars of family living left by Johnnetta's predecessors, reminding me of the ambiguous meaning of home. Home is the main workplace for many women; it is a refuge of relaxation for very few. For Johnnetta, Reynolds Cottage is a public place within which she has shaped a few spaces of privacy. The long downstairs living room is for formal entertaining; across the hall there is a more intimate sitting room, decorated with African art. The furniture of the dining room, gleaming inlaid antiques donated by a member of the Rockefeller family a generation ago, has given way to Johnnetta's own mahogany family pieces. Johnnetta's private study is tucked under the eaves.

I was struck by the similarity between the floor plan of this house and the floor plan of the president's residence at Amherst College, built at approximately the same time. Every college campus across the country is a crystallization of ideas not only about education but also about the basic relationships—family and class—within the society. The furniture that belonged to Johnnetta's black bourgeois parents in Jacksonville, Florida, will fit these rooms at Spelman, but it will be a complex task in this house to define a lifestyle that can fit the aspirations of young black women in today's America. At Amherst, I used to puzzle about the assumptions that lay behind the presentation of the college presidency, supported both by servants and a "first lady of the college" who arranged the flowers and place cards for dinner parties and worked as a volunteer (although she was professionally qualified) in the campus art museum. It seemed an example of sad insensitivity for a coeducational institution to hold up a model of a lifestyle that could only be achieved in a society of affordable servants and dependent wives.

One of the things that haunted me while I was at Amherst was the different meanings of "work" and "home" that hide behind what is becoming a false dichotomy for many men and women. The daily walks back and forth between my office and the college-owned house where I lived and the effort to harmonize my work in each made the notion of homemaking newly mysterious and provocative. Amherst College has a committee that is responsible for deciding many issues, including making decisions on tenure and promotions. During the fall semester, this committee is always overloaded, meeting for four or five hours at a time. These meetings were especially burdensome for me, since as dean, I had the responsibility of recording the deliberations, getting up at five the morning after a meeting to prepare the minutes before the rush for boots and oatmeal and the escaping school bus. Eventually, the committee would be driven to meet in the evenings; then, I would find myself at odds with my colleagues who preferred to take a two-hour break at home. I preferred to share a quick working supper that might allow us to adjourn at ten rather than eleven at night.

My main concern was not when the meeting ended, but with the oxymoron for me of going home to relax. Going home for most of my colleagues meant putting up their feet, relaxing with a cocktail, having a meal served to them. Going home for me meant dealing with domestic emergencies and desperately trying to help with Latin homework in the kitchen while preparing a meal. For most women and for increasing numbers of men, home is a workplace, often for a second or third shift in a single day. It is still immensely difficult for a woman with a family to make the moment of walking through the front door a moment of release. There is real work involved in housekeeping, in providing food and shelter, but even if we learn to minimize the mechanics of these jobs, the tasks of homemaking cannot be eliminated for their value goes beyond the mechanical. We enact and strengthen our relationships by performing dozens of small practical rituals, setting the table, making coffee, raking the lawn—giving and receiving material tokens, even in a household of servants. I entertained steadily in that house in Amherst, as if the passing of wine and cheese could repair the erosion of trust and intimacy that had happened at the college during the previous decade.

Marriage creates work, far beyond the apparent practical need, in order that work may create marriage. Couples rely on real tasks and shared effort or, lacking these, they invent endless elaborations of unnecessary tasks to assure themselves that their relationship and their need for each other is real, to knit it together from day to day. Women living alone, men living alone, even women and men heading households with young children get the practical chores done, but they do less housework than women living with husbands. If you compare statistics on different types of households, you find that the presence of an adult male means more additional work for the woman than the presence of a child under ten, even when the man believes himself to be sharing the housework equally.* What is not usually pointed out is that it is the aggregate work that is increased by marriage. It is not that males generate more laundry or dirty dishes or exude far more than their share of the fuzz that accumulates under beds but that new tasks are created by standards and expectations.

My husband and I live in an apartment in Cambridge, but increasingly I do my serious writing in our studio in New Hampshire, a single room with a loft, perched over a stream. When I am working alone, I throw together a meal and eat it in half an hour. My husband does the same thing when he is alone in Cambridge. But when we combine forces, working in the kitchen side by side, an hour is not nearly enough—it will be two hours before we have finished our meal. It's nicer and it's a better dinner, but we don't seem able to control it; as a result, both of us prefer to be alone when we have intensive work to do. The high points of Johnnetta's life

*Heidi I. Hartmann, "The Family as the Locus of Gender, Class, and Political Struggle: The Example of Housework," *Signs: Journal of Women in Culture & Society* 6(3): 366–94 (1980).

have been the weekends spent with her sons or the time spent courting with a childhood sweetheart in Washington, but she wonders out loud whether she could possibly live her present life if she were making a home for her menfolk day in and day out, even with domestic help.

It's hard to define the minimum needed to provide a sense of home sufficient to sustain relationships and growth, especially in this society of material opulence in which we generate endless hours of needless work to cancel the savings offered by technology. I struggle to be a homemaker without being drawn into the wasted labor of most housekeeping. Many people have pointed out that the introduction of computers in offices, though it may increase productivity, does not tend to reduce labor. This is not news: the pattern has been obvious for over fifty years, ever since the mechanical washing machine was used not to reduce time spent doing laundry, but to make it possible to change sheets and clothing two or three times as often. In the last ten years, the pressure has been rising to use up the gains of convenience foods by an elaborate gourmandise. We are a restlessly busy society, with little capacity to loaf in the sun (though we work hard at getting tans) or laze in bed (where "joy" is a serious obligation). We are as bullied by the obese Sunday paper as our New England ancestors were by two-hour sermons. There is some hope that even as the traditional distinction between home and work, which was elaborated to justify sharply divided gender roles, gives way before new kinds of family life, the distinction between work and leisure will also shift. The maintenance of relationships and refreshment of spirit associated with home and leisure are surely frontiers for the world of work, while more and more kinds of challenging effort find their way into off-duty hours. Increasingly, during the years of being a working mother and searching for quality time with my daughter, I have become convinced that the best times actually occur in the kitchen or the car, when some simple task like shelling peas or getting to the supermarket defines the time and space in which to build and strengthen our communication.

Relationships need the continuity of repeated actions and familiar space almost as much as human beings need food and shelter, but it is not clear how much food and shelter must be elaborated. I have always been moved by Elizabeth Marshall Thomas's description of the temporary homes the Bushmen build during periods of frequent moves through the Kalahari Desert.* As is true anywhere, there is a need for shelter; desert temperatures may drop below freezing at night. This need is met by a shallow concavity scooped out of the ground and lined with grasses. There, body warmth can be sheltered from the wind and conserved by a piece of hide. But such a shelter cannot be considered a home, even for a night, unless it has a hearth and an entrance as well as space to lie. The alignment of these establishes the internal order needed for privacy and propriety, and distinguishes the woman's side of the fire from the man's side, to keep elemental forces sorted out for the health of the community and success in hunting. For the Bushmen, a curved branch, leaning sideways, one end embedded in the

*Elizabeth Marshall Thomas, *The Harmless People* (New York: Alfred A. Knopf, 1959), 40–41, 196, 221.

ground, is the necessary minimum to define an entrance. The arrangement of concavity, hearth, and doorway orders the common activities of a household; it defines the home. When people live together, the high purposes of that common living, including the binding and the freeing of each, become expressed in very concrete details. The details vary, and we can experiment with changing them as we wish, but material tokens are a necessary part of those relationships.

All human groups share food in one way or another, often using different kinds of food differently. The Bushmen share the roots and nuts gathered by the women within the household, while they divide the game killed by the men among the larger community of the band. But not all human groups use the ceremony of eating together to establish and maintain relationships as we have tended to do in the Western tradition, and as we have elaborated in our Eucharists and Seders and wakes. The Passover Seder is an elaboration of the institution anthropologists call "commensality," eating at a common table. The rituals of the Seder echo the function of other family meals in defining relationships and reaffirming and passing on tradition, but this is not true for all cultures. A young American woman who went to Manus Island in New Guinea with my mother was scandalized to see her taking her meals alone and not inviting the villagers to join her at the table, convinced she had discovered evidence of racism. But my mother explained that even a traditional Manus feast did not involve eating together, but rather offering gifts of food to be taken home: families and friendships were not defined by shared meals.

It is not necessarily ominous that the formal family dinner is declining in many households or becoming limited to special occasions. We might be better off if we could separate food as nourishment and pleasure from food as the currency of care that leaves so many woman laboring long hours to prove affection in that semantic muddle called nurturance. There is a splendid lesson to be learned from the elaborate labor involved in infant feeding during the forties and fifties—the sterilization, the equipment, the rigid schedules—before the rediscovery of the simplicity of the breast. The ideal is to find simple forms that can be elaborated for delight or turned into art rather than onerous obligations. But the giving and receiving of these simpler material tokens of caring will still be essential.

As I began to think about the lives of the women in this project, I was struck by the diversity of their homes and the spaces they had created to live and work, by these concrete expressions of who they are. Joan is the only one of us who has spent long periods of her life as a traditional full-time homemaker. I have visited the Eriksons in at least half a dozen of their houses across the country. Joan talks about the sense of light and openness she tries to achieve for Erik, and I recognize familiar brightly colored pieces of art and handicraft from one house to the next, but they are always artfully recombined, each object at rest in its new place. Of all us, Joan has the clearest understanding of how objects that enrich the senses can also enrich human relationships.

It is possible to create a context of sharing with very simple material cues. This idea is best expressed by the old notion of sacrament. This word has been shaped and often abused by the Christian tradition, but it is still useful to express an idea that occurs in many cultures: that the most ordinary materials, like bread and clay, as well as those that are rare and shining, are carriers of meaning, and that the proper actions taken with these materials, around the day and the calendar, have a transformative value. The old Anglican catechism defined a sacrament as "an outward and visible sign of an inward and spiritual grace." I prefer the statement that turns up in some Catholic theological discussions: "a sacrament *effects* what it signifies."* The lighting of Sabbath candles, the giving of gifts, the preparation and sharing of food—all have the potential to bring about human closeness, as well as simply referring to it.

When my husband and I visited his family in Beirut on our honeymoon I was frustrated to find that my courteous and highly educated in-laws answered me in English whenever I spoke to them in Armenian. Then, on the fourth or fifth day of our visit, his mother set out to make *chee kufta,* a dish in which finely ground lean lamb is kneaded at length with bulgur wheat, parsley, and onions until the raw meat simply disappears into the wheat. It's one of those dishes, shaped by their mothers' hands, that sons go home to eat. Greatly daring, I went into the kitchen and took over the kneading. After that day, my in-laws began to answer me in Armenian, the handling of meat and grain and the sharing of what I had prepared having transformed me into a differ-

Enchiridion Symbolorum: Definitionum et rationum de rebus civii et morum, 33rd edition, ed. H. Denzinger. Freiburg: Herder, 1965. Nos. 1606, 1639.

ent person, just as the mother of a new priest is suddenly shy with her son after he has been touched with sacred oils, just as desire becomes holy after the exchange of wedding rings.

For most of us, the extraordinary superstructure of symbolic meaning created by money—money far removed from its connection with the beads that Joan has studied, or shells or gold, no longer even used for decoration, but instead spun off into mythic systems of abstract debit and credit, leveraged to monstrous proportions—has become a self-contradictory paradigm for the corruptions of materialism. Ironically, the notion of sacrament is both more material and more abstract than the notion of money or wealth. Money, which represents so many possibilities, becomes impersonal as it passes from hand to hand until it is reembodied in the shared comforts and conveniences of life. We have all been lucky in never facing severe poverty, but each of us uses these tangible symbols differently in shaping our lives.

There are vast differences in the way material tokens are used in ordinary life. Alice talked about the experience of poverty in postwar France, where people would share food and somehow, even during periods of scarcity, the food was tasty and the conversation good. She compared it with life in Baltimore when her father was unemployed, with the focus on those possessions that would not be shared from person to person. "It was very different from not having money in Paris. In Paris someone would always help, but here it was much colder. Even in the academic environment, we're a little more materialistic and don't exchange things so readily. People would discuss the prices of furniture or dishes without offering to help. And I thought the cooking was abominable."

Sharing is sometimes more demanding than giving; Americans often find it difficult to tolerate the level of interdependence involved in carpooling or sharing a laundry room in an apartment building. My efforts to stretch resources at Amherst by promoting sharing and interdepartmental cooperation were regarded as both galling and sinister.

Specific everyday tasks can be life-giving, binding individuals to each other and to the past. They can also be opened up as areas of choice, becoming the building blocks of identity. The immense diversity of foods and labor-saving devices available in America today have transformed food preparation for the affluent from a survival skill to a form of self-expression, obscuring the basic fact that human survival depends on the transformation of foodstuffs after their original production in agriculture. Almost all of the great staples of human nutrition, particularly the grains, are edible only after processing. In many parts of the world, the growing shortage of cooking fuel is almost as much of a threat to life as shortages of food itself.

The bountiful sharing of food on community occasions was central in the southern black community in which Johnnetta grew up. The fried-chicken feast that followed the Sunday service forms a single narrative strand with the preaching that made people "get happy," with the stamping feet and the familiar hymns. Yet, with this enjoyment of festive eating, formal daily eating was not emphasized in southern black culture, even in Johnnetta's middle-class family, where all members of the family worked hard outside of the home.

Barkev and I are old fashioned in our handling of the evening meal, beginning with an Armenian prayer and passing around serving dishes. My daughter's teenage friends would comment in amazement at the idea of a family sitting down to eat together on a daily basis in a room with no television. When Barkev and I first met, he was painfully thin. He had been living alone and away from home for nearly five years, earning his keep working the multiple odd jobs available to foreign students. He had even sent money home when his family, like many Armenian families, moved from Syria to Lebanon in the heightened tensions that followed the invasion of the Sinai and Suez in 1956. It was almost irresistible for me to combine my effort to relate to him by learning about Armenian language and culture with an effort to feed him. The outcome was that I learned Armenian cooking and committed myself to almost a decade of chopping and elaborate preparation, hours of packaging foods inside of other foods—grape leaves stuffed with rice, cheese folded in dough, even meatballs stuffed with a different meat mixture. I learned to cook almost entirely from a cookbook put together by the women's group of an Armenian church, and used lamb and rice as my staples. Ground lamb was three pounds for a dollar, but we spent the money saved on olive oil and pine nuts.

It took me a long time to move away from the more laborious dishes in the Middle Eastern cuisine, which really only make sense when there are a number of women in the household working and gossiping and caring for children side by side, dishes that become a form of servitude in the kind of American household where a woman is alone in the kitchen. In retrospect, I am shocked at how easily I discarded my mother's ingenious formulas for feeding me and entertaining guests. Her advice when I got married was to keep a soup pot simmering on the stove so the house would smell of home cooking without too much time spent in the kitchen—the symbol of loving effort without the hassle. The elaborate Christmas Eve dinners with which I replaced her steak and asparagus and green salad were duly praised by our friends, but they took a week to prepare.

After we had spent two years in the Philippines, where we had a cook, I never resumed my newlywed standards. I began to branch out with simpler European recipes, even adopting beef and potatoes, a momentous change. When I first knew Barkev, he joked about beef as "poor man's goat." For years, to express my need to go out and escape from our domestic pattern, I would say that I "needed a baked potato," instead of our usual rice pilaf. When we moved to Iran, our eating pattern changed again. Persian cuisine belongs to the same broad Middle Eastern tradition as Armenian, but instead of packages, most foods are combined in stews and sauces that often include fruits as well as meats and vegetables. At that time, Tehran boasted only a single, very expensive, Chinese restaurant, so I decided to learn Chinese cooking, which would give us back a contrast between my own cooking and the Iranian food we ate outside. After a trip out of the country, my luggage would contain fresh ginger and oriental spices as well as seasonal reminders of home like candy corn and cranberry sauce.

Today, Barkev joins me in the kitchen, sharing a drink and stirring a mean wok, and we start cooking when both of us are ready. It's a way of asserting that if all this effort is about relationship, that's what it ought to be, a reshaping of the chores of housekeeping into the rhythms of homemaking. This means that the nature of homecoming is changed for him, as it has changed for the husbands or lovers of each of the women I talked to. The experience of going home to relax has been altered. We may both sit down and watch the news, but there is no one making dinner while we do so. And I struggle, particularly when I am writing and my professional life is centered in the household, to resist the temptation to chip away at my workday by spending extra time on meal preparation.

This is still very different from my mother's approach to domesticity; it was sought out as innovation rather than passed on as tradition. My mother invented simplifications and economies of time; I have escaped tedium by incorporating the processes of learning and experimentation. I theorize about cooking, serve newly invented dishes to guests, and frustrate my family's desire for affirmations of the familiar by being unable to replicate last week's successes.

If you don't inherit a cuisine, as is the case with more and more American women, the nature of cooking changes. Newly learned recipes do not specify the gender of the cook, calling for "one maiden aunt, one hungry husband, one young wife desperate to please" along with the flour and oil. In order for Barkev to move away from patriarchal expectations of being served and not helping in the kitchen, it may have been necessary for us to discover a cuisine that was foreign to both of us. For those with cosmopolitan palates and ample incomes, the alternative to convenience foods and take-out is the culinary upward mobility of the eighties. Either approach is a way of redesigning food preparation so that men are willing to participate.

For Alice and Jack, gourmet cooking was not a solution but an end in itself. The natural environment of their relationship was the kitchen. Every person of importance to Jack was invited to join in, first in companionable kibitzing around the kitchen table while an array of white wines and interesting hors d'oeuvres appeared as the preparation lengthened, and later as we sat down for the full feast. Deeper layers of friendship involved sharing the search for ingredients or the reduction of sauces after the baking of bones and herbs in the oven. By his enthusiasm, Jack inspired an interest in cooking in both men and women, although cooking was not a new interest for Alice, for whom it is the continuing affirmation of a European identity. What would once have been exotic now fits. Not surprisingly, food was carried from the Riverbend household to the labs and offices of Demonics. After Jack's death, Alice continued to use food to symbolize the working relationships she was trying to promote, setting a table of delicacies at Christmas and organizing an elegant catered dinner when the company went public.

In the nineteenth century, a young woman named Ellen Richards, trained in chemistry and unable to work in her field, announced the foundation of a new science she called oekology, or the science of living. This was the discipline later called domestic science or home economics, involving the effort to professionalize and dignify the work of the housewife by drawing on science and technology.* A single Greek root, *oekos,* has wandered through changing conceptions of human living, as well as changing fashions in spelling, producing the contemporary fields of economics and ecology, which frequently seem to be at odds. It also offers the less well-known term ekistics, coined by the city planner Constantinos Doxiadis to refer to a science of human settlement that would include the architectural creation of human spaces, their social and economic integration, and their relationship with the natural environment. Each of these latter-day coinages represents an incomplete view, but together they represent a view that includes biology and architecture, kitchens and stock exchanges, the growth of meadows and children as well as the GNP. In every case, we can visualize ourselves as consumers or as old-fashioned husbands who expect to be served, or we can take a share of responsibility for every-day life as a sustainable weave of effort and enjoyment which builds up rather than breaking down.

What we need today is not to apply more technology to housework, or even to teach those who do housework to avoid nonbiodegradable detergents or aerosols. We must transform our attitude toward all productive work and toward the planet into expressions of homemaking, where we create and sustain the possibility of life. It may take yet another new word to express the single responsibility that unites the homemaker, male or female, with the men and

*Barbara Ehrenreich and Deirdre English, *For Her Own Good: 150 Years of the Experts' Advice to Women* (Garden City, NY: Doubleday Anchor, 1979), 153.

women who mine and plant and create industries and work for effective forms of exchange and for a peaceful world. Such a new term might be *ecopoiesis,* using the Greek root for *making* that gives us the word *poetry.* Still, the making of words or rhymes is insufficient; the problem is with our understanding of the materialities that make life possible: the forests and the cooking pots, the necessary recuperation time of fields and workers, the private spaces of our lives where the spirit flourishes, and the woodlands that are still wild.

CARETAKING

WHEN I WAS STAYING WITH JOHNNETTA, we would get up while it was still dark, put on shorts and running shoes, and do stretches and warming-up exercises on her front porch before setting off for an hour of energetic walking. Johnnetta was determined that if she was to be set visibly in the middle of the Spelman campus, one of the ways she would serve as a model for the students was to precede the dawn with physical exercise. We would start out by walking around the campus and then, with first light, go through the gate into the black neighborhood beyond, through one of the country's earliest housing projects, which was separated from the young ladies of Spelman by a tall chain-link fence. Later, we would get an hour of interviewing done, and then

Johnnetta would go to her office while painters and movers came in and out of the presidential mansion, displacing my work from room to room as I transcribed tapes.

On Thursday, after we finished our morning session, Johnnetta left for New York to supervise the removal of furniture from her Brooklyn apartment and her office at Hunter College and to send two of her three sons off to visit their father, who was working in Zambia. On Friday, word came that she would be delayed. Late that night, she called and explained that her youngest, Che, had been hospitalized for an emergency appendectomy, and she would stay in New York at least until he was well enough to bring down to Atlanta. Of all her current commitments, I was the most portable, so I came to New York. We continued our walks on the streets of Brooklyn and our tapings in the partly dismantled apartment, while Johnnetta visited Che in the hospital and dealt with a *New York Times* interview. Johnnetta had all sorts of backup arrangements ready in New York, but as she said, "Somebody's got to be the mommy." In our society, it's usually the mother who has to be the mommy, whatever other responsibilities she may have.

The first week I was at Amherst as dean of the faculty, while I was going through the same process of unpacking and arranging in the evenings and trying in the daytime to find my way into the stacks of papers left by my temporary predecessor, my ten-year-old daughter Vanni had a biking accident that resulted in a concussion. At the hospital they said I could take her home, but that I should check her pupils once an hour through the night. The next day, she was pronounced fit to travel, and we drove to Cambridge to greet my husband. He was returning from a trip to Europe after having injured his leg in a sailing accident; he needed another emergency-ward visit and two days of nursing in bed. How many women can tell the same story of a sudden demand for caretaking? And how often does that demand crop up not a month or a year into a complex new role, but within the first few days, during the window of accident-proneness that seems to accompany every upheaval in family life?

The caretaking has to be done. "Somebody's got to be the mommy." Individually, we underestimate this need, and as a society we make inadequate provision for it. Women take up the slack, making the need invisible as we step in to fill it. The ethologist Konrad Lorenz used to talk about the number of eggs laid by the same species of songbird when nesting at different latitudes. As you go farther north, the hours of daylight in summer are longer, so a given parental pair could gather food adequate for a larger number of fledglings. As you go south, the available daylight decreases, as does the average number of eggs. For the songbirds, surviving and raising the next generation fill the entire day. What is amazing about humans is that we seem able to do so much else; yet much of what we do is caretaking in another form or involves tasks that would be done better if they were understood in that way.

In this society, we habitually underestimate the impulse in men, women, and even children to care for one another and their need to be taken care of. In a multiplicity of forms, caretaking is part of the composition of almost every life. Because we have so elaborated the caretaking professions, we may not notice the amount of caretaking done by an artist with apprentices or by a chief of engineering or a college president; we fail to notice the aridity of these jobs when they do not involve care for others. A. A. Milne, in the nursery rhyme, understood the impulse in a three year old, "James James Morrison Morrison," to take care of his mother, but we are largely blind to caretaking by children and often miss the mutual caretaking of men in mines and foxholes. When Johnnetta walks in the morning, she is taking care of herself by dealing with the stress that goes with her job and taking care of her students by giving them a useful model. She is also caring for an idea, the idea of young black women striding out into their lives, limber and free. Coming to New York to care for a hospitalized son could be seen as a distraction from her professional commitment, but in fact it provides a symbolic refocusing of the other kinds of care, a style of response and commitment learned over a lifetime. Being a mommy is part of being a good president.

Ellen is the only one of the women I worked with who formally belongs to one of the caretaking professions. Our conversations often turned on alternative modes of caretaking, especially during the months when she was reconstructing her professional life around the care of a first and then a second child. Even the field of psychotherapy is divided on issues of how much care is needed and when, who may give it and what can be achieved by it. When Ellen was practicing as a psychotherapist, she was seeing patients once or twice a week, but analysts often see patients daily. Psychoanalysis is an intensive, skilled, and very expensive form of care or training; one of the principal thrusts in mental health has been to find briefer and less labor-intensive forms of treatment.

It struck me, talking to Ellen, that the number of patients an analyst can treat intensively is not that different from the number of family members a full-time homemaker can care for. The model on which the traditional family is based is comparable to the most expensive and intense forms of professional care we have in our society, but it leaves out a readiness and a responsibility to take care of others that is spread throughout society. Johnnetta doesn't need to be imprisoned by the care of one family, for her care and commitment reach more widely. But the particular commitments within her family inform everything else she does. She joked that there would be some in Atlanta who would be reassured to hear she was in New York with Che; she simultaneously wondered whether the same people would hold it against her.

How much care is needed and how much human effort needs to go into caretaking? There is no way to compute it, for the meaning of the word "care" is endlessly ambiguous: it has one meaning in a hotel and another in a hospital, one in a day-care center and another in a university. There are different needs for care between infants and adults, healthy and well, and great differences are made by training, skill, and equipment. Part of our blindness comes from the fact that in some situations, the need for care is urgent because of accident or earlier neglect; in others, invisible care routinely given has meant that no need is ever apparent. Any computation of dollars or numbers for such a spectrum is nonsense, but the image of the songbirds stands as a reminder that caretaking is essential to survival, while the connection between the number of eggs and the hours of daylight poses a question of the underlying mathematics of human caring. For human beings, "caring for" means far more than hunting for worms for a nestful of squawking fledglings; it emerges in every activity, from electrical engineering to bookkeeping to farming.

Today, we all risk being without needed care at some crucial moment, or of suffering from the effects on others of insufficient care. At one time, many men could assume that their wives would devote their lives to caring for them and their children; the elderly could once count on the care of their adult daughters and sons (or the sons' wives). Now, the problems of giving and receiving needed care force everyone to improvisation and patchwork. For all our elaboration of professional forms of caretaking, caretaking is necessarily dispersed through the society. It is a skill that everyone can usefully learn, practiced mutually, necessary both in the workplace and at home, and no longer attached to a fixed set of roles. When Joan and I were taping interviews, Erik developed a ritual of bringing us tea—caring for us but also soliciting care, checking in with Joan for reassurance about the plans of the day.

Homemaking can be done in tandem, but caretaking, even when two people alternate, is always a complementary relationship, never exactly symmetrical. One hopes that in a marriage the times of greatest need will not coincide, that when the one is most needy the other will find resources. But these rhythms of give and take are not easy to develop. Even at the dinner table, it takes skill to allow both partners enough of what my husband calls emotional air time to recite the troubles of the day and be comforted; it is harder still when the needs of the whole week must be compressed into a weekend. It can only work if each partner learns to find satisfaction in caring for the other, like learning to enjoy the mutual giving of pleasure in the syncopated rhythms of lovemaking.

We have also become increasingly thoughtful about the question of self-care. Some of this is fashion, some of it can be dismissed as narcissism or a new way of expressing affluence, but some of it is an investment in autonomy and in sustaining the quality of life through a longer maturity. We joke about women who urge their men, like children, to wear their galoshes or to get needed exercise, but it is a vast relief when these same men start to take some responsibility for their own well-being. Just as important, women need to care enough about themselves to care for themselves as more than the property of some man.

It is not easy to learn to cherish oneself when one's life has been organized around cherishing others or when all the cherishing has been delegated to someone else. During my Amherst years, on the weekdays of coming home to a single-parent household, I felt a weary envy of my predecessor, who had a full-time homemaker waiting for him. I justified the time I put into developing an exercise program or learning about computers by what these pleasures would enable me to offer the college. Still, I used to buy flowers and silk scarves as tokens of caring for myself and treat myself to long scented baths with the phone turned off. Alice lives alone since Jack's death and it is all too easy for her to treat her vacations as expendable when they are not justified by the needs of others. We all need someone to cherish and be cherished by.

Today, those who begrudge themselves care, feeling that their role in life is to care for others, can be persuaded to think about issues of health and stress reduction. As a result, a little cherishing of the self is translated into responsible behavior, even a way of caring for others—like Johnnetta's exercise walking. But self-care is important for its own sake as well. It is intimately tied to self-esteem, with the implication that the one who is cherished is important and valuable for his or her own sake.

Ellen has always moved between the issues of caretaking that accompany privilege and those that arise at the point of desperation. She was working as director of the psychiatric emergency service at Beth Israel Hospital when emergency wards, set up to deal with accidents and sudden emergencies, began to be flooded with patients with chronic complaints whose disrupted lives gave them no regular access to care. The appearance of the homeless on the streets of America is a visible reminder that while some Americans receive the most expensive and skilled forms of care, from organ transplants to psychoanalysis, others may be entirely alone and uncared for. The situation demands both new definitions of need and new institutions and highlights the fact that obtaining care is a skill. There is a necessary spectrum in which a commitment to care for the desperate balances the commitment to provide intimate care within the household. Together, the two offer a perspective for creating a society adequately cared for. Every time we turn away from including compassion in the national agenda, we handicap ourselves for real leadership.

Ellen has always done some individual psychotherapy, but she was also assigned as a resident to work at Boston State Hospital, a large state mental hospital, before deinstitutionalization. At the state hospital, psychiatrists spent more time resisting the constant threat of disorder than they spent on healing. As a result of this work, she came back to the Harvard University teaching hospitals far more knowledgeable about the use of medications in psychiatry than those who were clinically trained in more fortunate environments.

Ellen's mixed experience poses mirror questions, not contradictions. What is the finest level of care that can be given to an individual—and how can thin resources be stretched farthest? Even more complex, when is it justifiable to give substandard care because this is preferable to no care at all—and when does this court the risk that substandard care may be institutionalized, that a group of professionals may acquire a vested interest in maintaining it? Beyond these questions lies the issue of when and how standards can be made to converge and how individuals in need can be strengthened to the point of being able to care for others— and indeed, as Alcoholics Anonymous has demonstrated, how caring for others becomes a source of strength.

In 1987, I went with Ellen and a group of her colleagues on a committee sponsored by the Institute of Medicine to visit several Boston-area shelters for the homeless. The program at these shelters ranged from almost one-on-one caretaking, designed to provide whatever support was needed to get individuals established in long-term independent living, to intensive utilization of resources designed to get as many individuals as possible off the streets and minimally cared for during the winter nights when they might otherwise freeze.

At one extreme, there was Project Hope in Roxbury, run by the Little Sisters of the Assumption, a teaching order. The sisters have adjusted to reduced numbers of vocations and changing neighborhood needs by retraining themselves and turning their energies and dedication to new activities. The old convent now functions as a shelter for homeless women and their children. We sat in the convent parlor and chatted with some of the guests: teenage mothers with children who had never had a home of their own, and divorced or never-married women with long histories of seeking affordable housing and struggling to make ends meet, camping with relatives or sleeping with their children in parked cars. "You can trace it back," Ellen said. "Before a family or individual enters the category 'homeless,' there has been a long history of difficult circumstances and uprooting, sometimes violence, often going back more than a generation, so that simply providing housing isn't enough. And you can see the depression and developmental deficits appearing in the children." It struck me that because having a home of some kind is a precondition for the other ways in which one generation cares for another, making growth possible, that homelessness almost has the look of a genetically transmitted disease.

The sisters at Project Hope attempt to address the full spectrum of problems—including problems with the bureaucracy and its intricate rules surrounding housing subsidies, welfare payments, the placing of children in schools with appropriate special programs, and so on. They try to maintain support as long as it is needed, working together in the handsome old convent with its bright kitchen and wonderful big playroom, and sharing childcare. The children seemed spunky and lively, grabbing the visitors' hands, asking our names and then showing us around, but the very friendliness made me uneasy, as if these children were urgently seeking adult response and warmth, even in this small facility with its very high ratio of caretakers. The sisters can accommodate no more than six or eight families at a time, a total of about twenty guests with some dozen adults devoted to caring for them and solving their problems, giving each family group at least a private room and a home address to which to return. But the program seems to work; within a year or so, a good percentage of long-term solutions are achieved, with families settled in apartments and even self-supporting, children achieving up to grade level in school, mothers able to care for themselves and their children. The most striking difference between homeless families and welfare families, both of them usually headed by females, is that substantially more of the homeless female heads of household came from *unbroken* homes, homes where men were present, although often abusive. Women who know how to survive in the welfare jungle often grew up in female-headed households—poor but not homeless—where women looked after women.*

*Ellen L. Bassuk, MD, and Lynn Rosenberg, ScD, "Why Does Family Homelessness Occur? A Case-Control Study," *American Journal of Public Health* 78: 783–788 (1988).

Family shelters like Project Hope are a recent phenomenon. When Ellen was doing her research at the Bunting Institute in 1983, homeless families were just beginning to turn up. She would come upon parents in the shelters, perhaps with a baby sleeping beside them in a cardboard box, mixed in with homeless individuals. As if moving backward in time, we went from Project Hope to the Pine Street Inn, one of the oldest and most famous of shelters for homeless individuals. It was designed to stretch resources as far as possible in order to meet urgent and short-term needs. Even so, resources are still not sufficient. Unlike Project Hope, which is a temporary home for periods of a year or more, Pine Street is a refuge for one day at a time. Every morning, the guests must leave and pass the day elsewhere. Even those who return will not get the same bed they had the night before. In the interval, all of the bedding will have been stripped and the empty rooms disinfected.

We arrived at about half past four, in time to see a line of men being processed slowly through the front door. A young woman frisked them efficiently and impersonally for weapons, drugs, or bottles; they then filed past a uniformed policeman in the entry. Outside, there was a small plaza where a few men lingered, finishing their bottles; this is a "wet" shelter, and they are not turned away if they check in drunk. The only concession to the desire for a home, as contrasted with a shelter for the night, is that guests can hire lockers on a monthly basis, but because the same guests do in fact come back night after night, workers and guests often greet each other by name. After entering, some men go to the clinic, where aspirins are handed out, wounds are tended, and swollen feet are soaked in antiseptic solution. "How are you today?" the attendants ask. "Let's see how that sore on your leg is doing." Other men line up immediately for meals donated by local restaurants.

I stood in the lobby trying to understand what I was seeing and what it said about changing standards and our increasingly interdependent lives. I grew up in a New York neighborhood where I learned to step around drunks on the sidewalk, to think of them as failures or dropouts whose predicaments were unconnected to me, rather than generated by the same social system that supported me. Today, less than a third of the shelter population have the familiar look of alcoholic derelicts, bleary eyed and red faced, marked and bruised by falls. A number of men look reasonably healthy and able, often quite young. These are men who have been economically uprooted, who are weathering some kind of transition in their lives. But the air of unpredictability in the room emanated from another group of men who seemed disoriented or who behaved bizarrely.

Five years ago, the administrators of Pine Street, like others dealing with the homeless, were adamant in insisting that homelessness was primarily an economic matter. Partly because of Ellen's work, it is now accepted that a large percentage of homeless individuals are mentally ill, including many deinstitutionalized long-term mental patients. These lost souls were often abandoned by their families during their years of incarceration, as they became less and less competent to deal with the mechanics of modern life or to form sustaining connections of any kind. They were then extruded from large public institutions on the assumption that they would be cared for by community public-health facilities, but the facilities were never built and the stabilizing medications ceased to be dispensed or supervised. Even as they draw comfort from routine and are glad to benefit from the shelter, there are too many different rhythms and too many people, men involved in fantasies at cross-purposes with one another, muttering and arguing with the empty air when their conflicts intertwine. Fights and arguments break out from time to time, and then one or more are removed— as several were delivered earlier—in a Black Maria.

After the meal, all those for whom there are beds must shower, stripping before entering the unpartitioned shower room where attendants watch for signs of body lice or infections that need treatment. Clothes are kept overnight in a heated room that kills vermin. A set of fans draws room air across ultraviolet lights turned toward the ceiling, in the hope of preventing the spread of drug-resistant TB. Pine Street Inn was once a laundry, and the upstairs sleeping area consists of huge loft-like rooms, surprisingly clean and free of the smell of urine or antiseptics, with row on row of cots. The donated bedding and linens reflect domestic fantasies of every kind—Mickey Mouse, rainbows, flowers, a riot of particularity in this impersonal space.

Homeless women are lodged in a separate and smaller part of the building, which is entered through a different door. Even the professional visitors are asked to move quickly and discreetly through this lobby. Ellen commented that many of the women, unlike most of the men, are upset if they feel they are being observed. There are fewer women than men, a sharper sense of dislocation. We saw no women who looked simply ordinary or ordinarily drunk. "It's a more disturbed group of women here than Rosie's Place or some of the other shelters that take women," Ellen pointed out. "Pine Street is a pretty daunting shelter for a woman to come to because it's a wet shelter and there are so many men." The women's section upstairs acknowledges the women's greater need for privacy; there are waist-high partitions around clusters of beds, curtains in the shower entries, and a multicolored supply of donated bathrobes.

Pine Street has had a tradition of never turning anyone away in bad weather. If all the beds are taken, latecomers are allowed to stay in the lobby and sleep on the floors and benches. Men who are unwilling to shower can also sleep downstairs. Recently, the Inn has acquired additional space so that in the future it may not be necessary to admit guests without providing beds, but anything is better than the street in a New England blizzard.

It is as if the goal of Pine Street were to make sure that these men and women are no worse off tomorrow than they are today; indeed, they start the next day clean of body and approximately free of vermin, having had dinner and breakfast and perhaps had sores or wounds treated or acquired a needed garment from donated supplies. The same night spent in the street might have meant illness or death by freezing or predatory human attack; women who sleep in the streets are raped again and again. But Pine Street (although it will direct guests to places where they can be treated for drug abuse or alcoholism) applies no pressure for reform. There are no pledges to take, no moral agenda to impose.

Caring for others, and even caring for oneself, always

involves commitment and always has a time dimension. Usually commitment goes in two directions. At Pine Street, the commitment of care is very brief and very primitive, hardly more than custodial, but it is still based on a notion of the value of persons and their freedom. The return commitment involves no more than observing a few simple rules of the house. Ellen referred to the Pine Street Inn as a "hi-tech shelter," emphasizing the hot rooms and ultraviolet lights and the techniques to prevent the transmission of infections among so many ill-cared-for bodies. But Pine Street is more accurately a mass-production shelter, efficiently providing a minimum for those who would otherwise have nothing. At Project Hope, the relationship is more complicated and longer lasting and is built around a concern for the children shared by the nuns and the homeless mothers. Project Hope has a complicated ethical agenda that suggests a way of being in the world—responsible and self-supporting, able to give care as well as to receive it.

The sisters divide the labor, but they live directly with their responsibilities, as parents do. "One of the things that internship teaches you," Ellen commented, "though it's funny that I would ever say anything that sides with being an intern, is what it means to take care of a patient. And what it means is that they need to be taken care of twenty-four hours a day. You learn that they are your patients and you are responsible. And, in some way, I think you really learn about illness, inside out and backwards and forwards, about what it means to the person, the family, the impact of all of it. Now, could you be confronted with that responsibility any other way? Probably. But I know one of the things that used to really rankle me was dealing with people taking care of patients who didn't understand that they were in it for the duration, twenty-four hours a day. Nursing training is based on this model too. Oh, you go off and on shift, but nurses know how to take care of patients. They know that they are absolutely responsible. Occasionally, you get social workers who are trained somewhat differently and think that care is only needed from nine to five. I used to have trouble with that." For Ellen, the conflict between motherhood and career came not from the macho hours demanded by ambition but from the challenge to provide direct and sustained caring in two different places.

When I was first thinking about going into administration, a male acquaintance commented on the pastoral role of a dean. One becomes an advisor, a keeper of confidences, and an advocate. The issues people would raise with me were personal as often as they were professional, and I became fascinated with the challenge of improvising solutions to problems, as well as trying to elicit the performance needed for the institution. This mixture of public and private is especially common in academic settings, where the majority of the faculty are like members of an extended family, condemned willy-nilly to see the same faces across the table for life. Caring for the faculty is vital to promoting their continuing growth, which in turn supports the growth and development of students. Still, there is very great variation in the way different administrators interpret their roles in caring for others. Ironically, although I spent a great deal of my time on caretaking, I was criticized for being "not consistently nurturant," although I have watched men in the same kind of role who are not even remotely nurturant. The appropriate degree of caretaking in such roles as dean can only be accessible to professional and conscientious men and women if it is freed from cliches and practiced with judgment: the best caretaker offers a combination of challenge and support, yet adults dealing with women administrators are sometimes as fretful as infants denied the breast. To be nurturant is not always to concur and comfort, to stroke and flatter and appease; often, it requires offering a caring version of the truth, grounded in reality. Self-care should include the cold shower as well as the scented tub. Real caring requires setting priorities and limits. Even the hard choices of triage have their own tenderness. Again and again in myths and folklore, kindness to strangers or animals is enjoined and heroes are rewarded for pausing on their journeys to care for those in need. But psychologist Jean Houston points out an episode in the myth of Psyche and Eros that provides a useful balance. When Psyche is in search of Eros, she is enjoined to resist the cries and pleas of others. If she is to find her beloved, she must harden herself against inappropriate impulses to help and nurture.

When I went to Amherst, I valued my pastoral role as dean as part of a complex web of responsibilities to faculty, students, and the long-term integrity of the institution. I had not foreseen that the stereotype of nurturance would be used as a weapon. It is a double-sided blade that is turned only against women: my colleagues were equally ready to condemn faculty women for being too nurturant, and for not being nurturant enough. I also had not anticipated the extra burdens that went with meeting the expectation of nurturance. The president, for instance, had a wife, several secretaries, and a personal assistant, yet he still demanded a disproportionate amount of caretaking. Although he wouldn't ask me to bring him cups of coffee or perform personal errands, he would ask me to support his morale, cover for him when he was unprepared, prevent his impulsive actions, and listen to him let off steam or think out loud for hours at a time. These were tasks he automatically expected of women, but he also demanded them, to a lesser degree, from the men around him. Yet he appeared to have no sense that he had some caretaking responsibility for his staff, who used to end up in my office, expecting me to nurse them back to self-respect. It took a lot of us to care for the president and keep him in good running order, at the cost of neglecting other responsibilities. Some of his need was a legitimate balance to the strains of his position; some of it was a habit of being indulged that made me wish parents could rear their children without such a core of neediness and without the expectation that others could be used to fill it.

Almost any activity can be interpreted at least in part as caretaking. One of the most striking aspects of the Eriksonian version of the life cycle is that the basic strength that characterizes the long adult years is the virtue of care. The achievements of maturity are described, for both men and women, in analogy with parental responsibility, including the willingness to relinquish control gradually and welcome the transition to an unknown future. At its best, care creates freedom. But even as almost any activity can be informed by care, the caretaking professions themselves can be distorted into forms of exploitation rather than caring, with one asymmetrical relationship easily transmuted into another. Caring fathers and mothers can become tyrannical patriarchs and matriarchs, devouring their children instead of nurturing them. Healing and helping can become forms of domination, medical qualifications an excuse for bullying. When Ellen first talked to me about shelters, I was amused at the euphemistic optimism of calling those driven to depend on them "guests." After I began to get a sense of the pain and vulnerability of the homeless, I began to see this terminology as a steady, careful reminder, against all evidence, of the value of respect and of the freedom to move on.

It's a curious alchemy, the way caring enters into and transmutes other activities. An interesting example is the Iditarod, the 1,157-mile dogsled race across Alaska that has been won repeatedly by a woman, Susan Butcher. This grueling course was first run to save lives at a time when serum was desperately needed in Nome to combat an epidemic. Now, as a race, the mode of caring and service has been converted into competition, but it is clear that even within the competitive framework, Butcher achieves excellence by conceptualizing the struggle in terms of caring for her dogs. At every rest stop in the 1987 race, her rival Rick Swenson left early, while Butcher gave her dogs the full four-hour rest time; she was so busy caring for them that she had only fifteen minutes of rest for herself. By the end of each lap, her dogs were forging ahead of his. "My dogs just kept getting stronger and stronger," she told the *Boston Globe* (March 20, 1987). "They gained in power the further along we got." At the last rest stop, the rules of the race required Swenson to give his animals the full rest time. Butcher's lead became unbeatable. Where he was willing to overtax his dogs, she was willing to overtax herself, organizing her efforts around caring for her dogs. After the race, care for herself: a glass of wine, a hot bath, and sleep. It has been observed that in women's athletics, the women will stop playing when a teammate is injured, until she has been attended to, while male athletes will more quickly resume their competitive combat. Slowing down for caretaking is obviously a losing strategy in the short run, but a winning strategy in the long run, whether in a two-week race across Alaska or the life and survival of the human species on a planet that must be cherished, for it can never be replaced.

It is easy to think of caring in terms of embrace and nurture, in the image of a mother holding a child, but Ellen spoke of caring in terms of a quality of attention, a total commitment to looking and listening, that also reminded me of Vanni's infancy. "To do therapy," Ellen said, "you have to be unencumbered, so you can really listen reflectively and allow your free associations to be very present in your head and not be all cluttered with other things." This quality of attention has the same paradoxical quality as the need to be on duty twenty-four hours a day: it cannot be perfectly achieved, but it proposes the ideal that underlies real caring. No one is more attentive than a mother trying to learn to recognize and respond to the needs of a newborn. She sleeps, of course, but she is sensitive to cries even when she is busy or sleeping. There is a sense in which we need to turn that same kind of attention toward the fields we cultivate and the organizations we manage if these charges are to thrive.

Growing up with the capacity to care for people or communities or ideas depends on the early experience of receiving loving and effective care. It is the lack of this experience that turns homelessness into a cross-generational disease. Caring can be learned, especially through the kind of total responsibility given to young doctors, but it requires a base of empathy built before internship or residency. Ellen sometimes found this base simply lacking. "It was my contention that you don't need to know a lot to work in the ER but you had to have some intuitive sense of how to take care of someone—that was always one of my hobby horses. In the ER you're at risk because they discharge people. Sometimes someone is discharged who is dangerous, really psychotic, and you wonder how the resident could possibly have missed it. Sometimes you have to follow a patient or hold their hand, and there are some people you just can't let walk out of there because you just know they are going right down the tubes. Some residents were fabulous caretakers and you never had to say another word, but some, no matter what you told them, they didn't have the foggiest idea about taking care of an ER patient. All you really needed to know was if somebody was in trouble. The rest was gobbledygook. Well, that's too reductionist, but there's an element of truth in that. I actually gave some residents a hard time around their inability to take care of people. The bottom line is that there are people who are good caretakers and some that you wouldn't want taking care of your horse."

Today there are many people who decide not to have children, but this decision does not need to mean turning away from caring, as it does not for the Little Sisters of the Assumption at Project Hope. A more important question is whether an individual has had the opportunities to practice caregiving that can provide a frame of reference for less direct kinds of caring in the future. Girls are encouraged to imagine themselves into maternal and caretaking roles; boys have less opportunity for this kind of exploration unless they have younger siblings. Once upon a time, too, the work that men did contributed directly to caretaking: hunting trips that took men away from their families had a very direct connection with the sharing of food, and the battles that men fought carried a direct sense of protection. Today, the associations between jobs done by men and women and their care for their families are more obscure.

There has been a great deal of discussion of the need for fathers to be more directly involved in childcare, but the actual division of labor will always vary from family to family according to the needs and abilities of the family members. Still, caretaking, in its many forms, can be part of the composition of every life, and it is important to give everyone the chance to learn to care for another. Some children learn to attend to the needs of others by having pets; parents learn from each other and from their sons and daughters, if they let themselves, garnering knowledge they will use long after the childbearing years; the childless can seek out children to spend time with, building an awareness that can flow over into their other relationships. Ellen and I both had children rather late, and both of us made a point of finding children to be friends with during our childless years. Alice has never had a child of her own, but she seeks out friendships with children, Jack's daughters and mine, and even younger children. With children she becomes involved in their fantasies;

listening to Alice talk to a teenager gives me a sense of how she supports and encourages her engineers and software designers.

As we look ahead to longer and increasingly discontinuous lives, through which we can expect to move, from place to place and from task to task, it is clear that the congruence of different tasks, the recognition that a particular skill can be applied in the new context, is what makes the transfer of learning possible. Attention and empathy are skills, rather than biological givens for all women. Caring can be learned by all human beings, can be worked into the design of every life, meeting an individual need as well as a pervasive need in society. We need attention and empathy in every context where we encounter other living beings, and we need them to foster and protect all that we care for, laboratories and factories as well as homes and neighborhoods, fields and woodlands as well as nations and the peaceful relations between them.

MULTIPLE LIVES

A ROW OF PORTRAITS of previous presidents of Spelman hangs on Johnnetta's dining-room wall. It begins with the faces of four unmarried white women, devout Protestant ladies from New England. Their lives represent the tradition that women must choose between careers and domesticity— the old idea that it is not possible to be both a good wife and mother and also a scholar or a leader or a creative artist, even though it may be necessary to be a laborer or a menial. But the forced choice between intimacy and achievement is not limited to women. The continuing insistence on clerical celibacy by the Catholic Church reflects a rejection of the body and its pleasures, but beyond that, it is one more version of the notion that no man (and certainly no woman) can serve two masters. The two presidents who preceded Johnnetta were black men with wives and families. By the time they were appointed, having a wife to act as official hostess was almost a precondition for the job.

But women often do serve many masters. One of the most famous works in Arabic literature is the ode of Imru'u l-Qays, a poem that I have loved since I first learned Arabic and began to dip into the ancient poetry. A traditional Arabic ode begins with a passage of nostalgic recollection of past felicity and romance as the poet contemplates the signs of an almost-obliterated encampment in the desert, and then uses a description of travel by horse or camel to move to the main business of the ode, which is generally political, praising a particular tribal group or leader. The manly man recapitulates the masculine theme of separation from the domestic scene and initiation into the world of men, the transition from comfortable closeness to women in childhood to an adult male world. Here again is the model of strength to achieve drawn from singleness of purpose, the metaphor of a journey used to describe life.

In later periods, when the early odes were imitated ad nauseam by literate court poets for whom the desert encampment was as much a literary device as the sylvan scenes and shepherdesses of eighteenth-century literature, these sequences became highly conventional. But Imru'u l-Qays composed and recited his lines before the form was fully fixed; in them he moves from an invocation of the deserted encampment to a series of romantic reminiscences. In the poem, he seduces a woman who is pregnant by describing to her other adventures, including one with a mother distracted during lovemaking by the cry—or perhaps only the sleeping murmur—of a young child in the same tent. "When he cried from behind her, she turned away to him with a half, and under me half of her was not turned" (Imru'u l-Qays, line 17).

Not a familiar erotic image in Western literature (neither is seduction during pregnancy); but the problem of lovemaking disrupted by a baby crying, even when the baby is in a separate room as we prefer in our culture, is a familiar one, as is the mixture of arousal and jealousy during nursing. Husbands may respond to fatherhood as a situation of rivalry, especially if their wives were full-time homemakers before becoming mothers, or they may respond with a warmth and commitment that embraces mother and child in a single picture. But it is the mother who has to divide her attention between father and child and between different children, the breast baby and the knee baby. She is the one who must unravel an arithmetic in which the addition of a second child need not subtract from the love available to the first. The problem is a familiar one, even for full-time homemakers, but it is especially painful for women who are working out new combinations.

Ellen has to sort out her priorities between childcare and professional work in a context where her pleasure is also complicated by sibling rivalry perhaps exacerbated by her multiple tasks, perhaps muted by the presence of other caretakers. "Danny really knows how to get to me," she said. "The other night, for instance, I'm putting Sarah to sleep, and he walks in and says, 'Put Sarah down and hold me.'

Then he had a temper tantrum. He's always very clear about what he wants. Finally I got furious at him. I was wrecked."

This quality of dividedness has always been part of women's role, long before we were trying to divide ourselves between a law office or a business and the home. The artificial sequencing of the day's schedule often makes the problem seem like an issue of time, but really it lies deeper. I reread the line from Imru'u l-Qays, and I can feel twenty years of divided attention in a painful twist and pull in my back, a confusion in the senses. Childhood rivalries are common enough, and Ellen's training is probably an advantage in balancing the needs of her two children. Having them is clearly a delight to her and an enrichment of her life, but she is still pulled in different directions.

"I don't think I have ever fully and completely dealt with all these double and triple and quadruple roles," Johnnetta mused. "I don't think I know very many people who have. Most of the time it works, most of the time I am not unnecessarily whipping myself with some form of guilt, but some of the time I am. I've come up with an arrangement for Che to stay in New York that's a little unorthodox, but as soon as there's a problem it says, what's going on here? why aren't you there twenty-four hours a day to be mommy? and the question is raised again."

Society defines what demands may be made on women, and they are expected to give way, even when the demands conflict. Before the availability of contraception, many women died as a direct or indirect result of multiple pregnancies, and the fear of conceiving yet another baby was one of the factors that limited women's enjoyment of sex. Men reached out, knowing what they wanted, and women gave way. In the film *High Noon,* the hero is applauded for refusing to be distracted from his duty as a marshal by his love for his new bride, but she abandons her commitment to nonviolence for love of him. Women have been regarded as unreliable because they are torn by multiple commitments; men become capable of true dedication when they are either celibate, in the old religious model, with no family to distract them, or have families organized to provide support but not distraction, the little woman behind the great man.

But what if we were to recognize the capacity for distraction, the divided will, as representing a higher wisdom? Perhaps Kierkegaard was wrong when he said that "purity is to will one thing." Perhaps the issue is not a fixed knowledge of the good, the single focus that millennia of monotheism have made us idealize, but rather a kind of attention that is open, not focused on a single point. Instead of concentration on a transcendent ideal, sustained attention to diversity and interdependence may offer a different clarity of vision, one that is sensitive to ecological complexity, to the multiple rather than the singular. Perhaps we can discern in women honoring multiple commitments a new level of productivity and new possibilities of learning.

Running a household is not a full-time task nowadays, but then neither are most jobs. The forty-hour work week means that no one with a regular job needs to be consumed by making a living, even as it allows for a range of consuming increments. It is possible with flexible hours to have two "full-time" jobs, say by working one job nine to five on weekdays and then driving a cab for four or five hours afterwards and all day on Saturday and Sunday. So although such a schedule is very demanding, it is not surprising that many women manage it, because they have no other choice. One of their jobs is called "work," and one is called "home." People without domestic responsibilities may spend comparably long hours on some other second activity, a hobby or a sport, politics or religion, or may waste them in traffic or on long commutes.

But these are jobs, not careers. No one who is passionately engaged in his or her work limits it for long to forty hours a week. Positions carrying the greatest challenge or responsibility are predicated on this assumption. It is often in the second shift or late at night at the office that the really creative work is done. People of talent and ambition do enough work for two and are unlikely to invest vast amounts of time in other activities. Anybody can live two lives—few can live three at once. You may be able to work secretly on a novel or plan a revolution after working one job, but you can hardly do so after two. And not after a job that demands double time.

The fact that many women work a second shift while their husbands work only one is deeply unfair. Our indignation obscures the fact that the difference between men and women is not that men work one shift and women two, but that women with jobs usually do not have the flexibility to decide what to do with that second shift, which is already committed. Women fortunate enough to have challenging careers or creative ambitions can put in ten or twelve hours a day and still have difficulty meeting the macho hours of their colleagues. If they must then go home to an additional shift, they find themselves struggling to live three lives of effort and striving, scanting each.

The five women in this book have always worked, but our work has had different meanings. Although most of us have been employed throughout our adult lives, the shape of our outside working day has varied, and we have few hobbies. We have had periods of concentrated work around the clock, as when Alice and Jack were fighting for survival or when Ellen was an intern; periods of part-time work like Johnnetta's first years in Pullman or the semester after my daughter was born; even periods of working a single outside shift, always combined with other responsibilities.

The rhythms vary. My mother used to quote a line in a letter written by Harriet Beecher Stowe, in which she says that she is not getting on very well with her novel "because the baby cries so much." My mother's comment was that the reason the novel goes slowly is not because the baby cries so much but because the baby smiles so much. In fact, the baby is engrossing whether she cries or smiles, and a new baby is likely to occupy a large part of one's attention for a period of years, even with a ready supply of helpers. Certainly one will advance more slowly on the novel, but the novel may differ in important ways. The style of attention that allows a housewife to hold the phone with one hand while she checks the pot with the other and watches the toddler playing across the kitchen may be a genuinely creative model.

Part of the confusion about whether different activities are competitive or mutually enhancing has to do with the fact that we all necessarily live in two different economies, one an economy of finite resources, the other an economy of flexible and expanding resources. In the economy of finite resources, an arithmetic of addition and subtraction applies, and all games are "zero-sum" games: if you spend time in the office, you are not spending that time at home; the money that goes to Paul cannot also go to Peter; if the father leaves all his land to his oldest son, there will be none for the younger sons. In the economy of expanding resources, the games are "win-win" games: the arithmetic is multiplicative, credit can expand indefinitely; a day of rewarding effort can send you home frisky and exhilarated; a change in technology allows the land to produce more. It is almost impossible to keep these two ways of thinking in focus. Each reflects important truth and dangerous error. Most people have temperamental preferences for one style or the other, but either, by itself, produces nonsense.

Classical physics has taught us that energy is finite and conserved, but when we use terms like "energy" in speaking about human potential, we are into another area entirely, full of confusion if the physical metaphor is followed too closely. Everything we do is necessarily limited by finite resources of physical energy, but we rarely test those limits, since the capacity to mobilize physical resources depends on psychic "energy," which might better be called vitality. One person can "energize" or "empower" another without any transfer of physical quantities. The energy to write this page is released by metabolizing food—it comes from my breakfast. But the "energy" to write this page depends on my state of mind, and such "energy" can come from a sunset or a remembered smile. During the worst periods at Amherst, when my day was filled by fresh relays of professors bringing their desires and demands, convinced that they had only to lean on a female dean to get what they wanted, I learned to keep books of art and poetry in my office, giving myself three- and five-minute breaks to look at an African mask or linger over a verse and be refreshed. Most of us run out of "energy" long before we run out of energy, but conversely it is possible to increase "energy" without eating more. An activity that affects vitality is not directly competitive or subtractive from other activities—on the contrary, it may enhance them.

Both economies are at work at the same time. Both kinds of arithmetic affect the experience of every individual. It is not possible to "have it all" because of the finite economy. There are only so many hours in the day, and no one can be in two places at once. But the potential value of any hour is variable. Sometimes, having more—or giving more—means there is more there. "For unto every one that hath shall be given and he shall have abundance; but from him that hath not shall be taken away even that which he hath" (Matt. 25:29). Fatigue may sometimes be an energy problem, related to biochemical depletion of various kinds; but much fatigue is really a vitality problem. "Supermen" or "superwomen" need nourishing breakfasts, of course, but the quality of the breakfast cereal is insufficient to explain how some people can work fifteen-hour days with increasing zest, while others stagger from one task to another. Once you notice that, you wonder why we have organized our society so that work that could be invigorating becomes depleting. This is as true of factory work as it is of housework. When women argue that going back to school or taking a job outside the home will not detract from their capacity to be homemakers, they are often proved right by infusions of vitality.

The problem can easily be seen in relation to exercise. On the one hand, physical effort can be depleting, leading to fatigue and even exhaustion; on the other hand, regular exercise leads to the feeling of having more available, a more efficient metabolism and a more alert mind.

Human sexuality operates by the same kind of double mathematics. We find arguments that sex can be subtractive and depleting, but there is evidence that sexuality is an important element in all creativity, perhaps in all productivity. Freud discovered the pervasiveness of sexuality in human life, beginning in infancy, and the waste and mental illness created by the repression or distortion of sexuality. But he betrayed his Victorian roots by tying his theory of creativity to sublimation, to the notion of creativity *instead of* sex. This idea is directly related to the metaphors from physics that underlie his psychology. If sexual "energy" is a finite quantity that is conserved like the energy of classical physics, then it may be dangerous to dam it up, but it could be redirected, say into building cathedrals, and it might be wasteful to squander it. If you believe in this strictly limited arithmetic, you will require cathedral architects to be celibate so they can focus their entire lives on the single task. This belief is likely to become part of a more general belief in specialization and narrow focus.

The female life cycle, with its dramatic shifts in capacity, provides multiple metaphors for the arithmetic of vitality.

Men don't bear or suckle babies, but they do have to draw on physical reserves in many other ways, and they can use these metaphors to understand other aspects of their lives. When you think about stretching to meet a challenge or growing to the measure of a task, pregnancy is an extraordinary symbol of possibility, a reminder of the surprises in human potential. Then, when a woman gives birth, her body, which has been mobilized for the demands of pregnancy and delivery, shifts gears again for lactation. Women need to learn to nurse, as athletes need to learn to run farther and faster, or as couples need to learn to make love. Nursing mothers build up gradually to a shared rhythm in which mother and infant form a mutually regulating pair: as the infant grows and suckles longer and more strongly, the milk supply increases. It is the possibility of increase keeping pace with growth that makes wet-nursing possible. Logically, it is this possibility that allows mothers to combine nursing with other activities or to expand their capacities in other ways. Unfortunately, breast-feeding, partly because it can now apparently be easily replaced by bottle-feeding, is often subverted or undermined.

At Amherst, I decided I had better learn some new techniques for handling the stress of the deanship, so I asked one of the coaches, Bob Williams, to help me get started running. I count that experience as one of the most valuable of the Amherst years, for many women of my generation slipped through school without effective physical challenges; stamina remains a problem for many of us. He taught me that I needed to start slowly, stretching and limbering unaccustomed muscles, since good intentions can collapse in the first week with sprains and charley horses. Once a rhythm is established, it needs to be built up gradually, so that the more you do the more you can do, but there is always the possibility of doing too much too soon. Susan Butcher has mastered the art of getting optimum performance from her sled dogs without wearing them down, so that with each day of the Iditarod they are stronger. This is the approach we need to bring to the sustainable use and care of fields and fisheries and forests.

Experientially, the fact that the more you do the more you can do—up to some limit that most of us never test—shipwrecks easily. Without guidance and support, many women give up on breast-feeding. The first week of an exercise program, especially one I tackle unguided, is enough to make me give up in despair, saying I "don't have the energy." If I ran a little too far in the morning, I would doze in the office; if I ran a distance that I had worked up to gradually, I would be wide awake all through those insane days that started before six and often lasted until ten or eleven at night. At middle age, the difference between enough and too much was very narrow and would have been easy to miss without guidance.

The limits on the human capacity for all kinds of exertion are clearly similar, whether it is the capacity for running, or making love, or nursing a baby. Each activity has a core set of physical limitations surrounded by a complex of hopes and habits and anxieties. These are cybernetic systems, where capacity over time is governed not by addition and subtraction but by a feedback system that has the capacity, within limits, to spiral up to greater productivity or downward to failure. Hamlet praised his mother's love for his father by saying she hung on him, "As if increase of appetite had grown / By what it fed on" (*Hamlet* I,ii,144). Indeed. His comment about the middle-aged queen contains a more general truth about human sexuality and also about creativity and self-confidence.

Just as the capacity for sex or nursing or exercise is not governed by an arithmetic of addition and subtraction, so the possibility of combining these activities should be looked at in terms of synergy rather than competition. Having an active sex life at night does not necessarily make a man or a woman less productive on the job, yet even sex can become difficult and laborious or be overdone. The self-reinforcing effect of exercise works within a certain range, which can be adjusted, but is always liable to be disrupted by extremes. When schedules become rigid, adjustment is impossible and the level of effort that can be sustained over time drops.

One of the things that has fascinated me during my interviews is discovering how many things the women in this project fit into their days. Ellen is the only one with pre-school children now, and she repeatedly described simplifying her life and reducing her commitments so that she can concentrate on caring for her son and daughter. But with a little probing, out comes a long list of activities, including joint projects with a number of women friends. In fact, Ellen did not so much reduce her professional life to have children as change the way that life was organized, learning to compose the disparate elements in novel and less rigid ways.

"From the time I hit the doors of medical school, my life had been structured. I knew what I was doing every day, and

I was very busy and had little space. And I remember one day having the realization—it was like an aha! experience—I'm not going to be able to work like this and have a child. And having some clarity that, if I were ever going to have a kid, I'd have to quit my job. And feeling like I really didn't want to give it up and being very torn. I also felt taken in by some of the feminist ideology. I know a lot of successful women doctors that seem to have a very adequate and happy home life and take care of kids and also work in that kind of setting, going to work every day early in the morning, and coming home late at night, and having full-time childcare, but knowing me, I just knew I couldn't do that. And I remember what a jarring experience that was. I remember thinking, they did it, but they must have had to pay some price for it, because there are just so many hours in the day. I was burning candles at ten ends already, between a full-time administrative position in the hospital, a full-time clinical practice, ongoing clinical research, and teaching. There were really four major areas. So something had to be given up. You know, when you are in your twenties and thirties, you don't think about the limitations of things."

Ellen gave up her administrative position as director of the psychiatric emergency service and most of her clinical practice. She increased her research and writing, picked up a number of consulting contracts, and has been increasingly involved in projects related to the homeless. The most important difference between her life then and now is that in escaping from a career track in which her rhythms were dictated from above, she has become able to orchestrate her own life.

"I still to this day have continuing conflict about work and my kids, but I've set it up in such a way that I can kind of ride with the conflict and play it out on a daily basis. If Danny or Sarah are having a rough month, I can spend more time with them and put things off a bit. The name of the game for me now is to ensure flexibility in my daily schedule. That seems to be very important. If you've got patients, it eliminates a degree of flexibility, because they own those hours. You know, I'd be with a patient in my upstairs office, and I'd hear Danny cry downstairs, and it really bothered me. I'm ambivalent about cutting way back on my clinical practice, and I may go back to it—not immediately, with Sarah still so little, but later. But, in the practical mechanics of my day-to-day life, it works out well not to have absolutely fixed hours, because things change every week."

Alice looks at the question of how women combine their various commitments from the point of view of an employer. "We've had several cases of women who have had children while working for us. One brings the baby to work, but there's also a very good day-care center nearby. There's one woman engineer who has plenty of money, but she can't not work, because she's a creative person who likes the things we're doing on image processing—the sort of work you can't do on your own, requiring equipment and contributions from other people. She's excellent and always finishes on time, so I don't care if she's in the office or working on a terminal at home, unless I need her for a meeting. It does mean it's harder for her to be a leader at the moment. When she was pregnant, she volunteered to be on a TV show about working mothers and was turned down as unsuitable."

"She wasn't sufficiently oppressed," I commented.

"Correct. She had the money for childcare, the company was giving her flex arrangements to work at home, and we have a maternal-leave policy. Too easy." A very different situation from that of thousands of women whose employers offer no flexibility, who are caught in a model that assumes that work shaped in response to multiple commitments must be inferior work.

Alice has often hired women for engineering jobs because she has found them more flexible than the available men, about ideas as well as hours. "When I had to do something perceived as not doable, I would opt to have someone to help me who did not have the impediments that the men had with regard to schedules and so on. At Harvard in 1968, when minicomputers were just becoming available and I wanted to switch over, most of the men were used to having grad students as slave labor rather than using computers, and they were just shaking their heads, saying that it couldn't be done. I couldn't afford a doubting Thomas. I needed someone who I knew had the competency level and the energy level, and we just needed to do it. There were two women I could think of—the one I asked had a baby. She was very fast and very competent and if we needed to work all night we just did it. One of the things I experienced about the men was they had these concepts of regular time—you thought between such and such hours—and that's a concept that I've never had. Subsequently, I got to know the head of the programming group at Harvard, and she was extremely competent too, with this ability to say how long it would take to get a job done and then just do it. I always went with people like that—some of them were excellent cooks, too—all of my strong friends like to eat. At Polaroid I didn't come across really strong women at my level, but Jack had given me a lecturing about mentoring, so I started to do it and spent time with young women engineers, and they did very well. They were smart, but they had to be pointed in the right direction. And they had to be given responsibility—that's the main issue." We are used to seeing a woman with a baby as handicapped by her need for flexibility; we're startled to find that given the freedom to shape her own hours, she may be more productive than someone whose effort is defined by fixed schedules.

Like Ellen, Johnnetta pursues many simultaneous activities, yet she too has recently rearranged her commitments, in order to concentrate on the presidency of Spelman. It doesn't make her any less busy. In fact, we all talk about our time as if it were a flower bed continually invaded by wildflowers that we are reluctant to pull out. Our days are reminiscent of Edna St. Vincent Millay's "Portrait by a Neighbour," even when we try to be most disciplined: "Her lawn looks like a meadow, / And if she mows the place / She leaves the clover standing / And the Queen Anne's lace!"

The basic model of women's traditional role has always involved the simultaneous tug of different tasks. Today, there may be long gaps between the period of caring for young children and the period of caring for aging parents, but these tasks overlapped when lives were shorter and childbearing went on longer. Obviously, it is possible to care for an infant and a bedridden elder simultaneously, to work for several hours a day at a carpet loom with an ear open for calls and only occasionally burn the soup. I've watched Betty Steele, the director of the Academic Computing Center at Amherst, working in exactly the same way, struggling with complex budgeting or programming problems, interrupted again and again by students asking for help. There is a heritage here of responsiveness and interruptibility. It was the same for Alice. As director of research at Demonics, she was surrounded by engineers focusing on resolving separate problems, but she was always aware of the larger whole, bringing her engineers back on track when they became trapped in blind alleys.

Certainly this quality of broadly focused concern and interruptibility enables some important skills and hobbles others. There are tasks that really do require extended narrow concentration, but there are others that require a willingness to shift gears rapidly and think about more than one thing at once. Corporations, institutions, even nations are sometimes led successfully for a time by individuals who focus on single goals, but this narrowness is destructive in the long term. It is like the problem of monocrops: researchers develop a genetically uniform strain of wheat or tomatoes to maximize some single characteristic and then arrange for the planting of unvaried acres of that crop—which could potentially be wiped out by a single plague.

Julian Gibbs, who was in his second year as president when I went to Amherst, was a man of dogged attention to one issue at a time. When he was worried about some issue— for instance, the recurrence of sexual harassment in Amherst's fraternities, which he had permitted to operate if they would admit women—he would raise that issue in whatever

179

setting he happened to be in, often in monologue form, not noticing that the other person had some quite different issue in mind. Julian was apparently an able theoretical chemist and had postdoctoral researchers working under him continuing his projects, but when he was involved in a critical stage of the research, he would keep a blackboard in his office, covered with diagrams and formulas, and lecture whoever came in. It was not much use being either the baby that cries or the baby that smiles, the president was preoccupied.

For me, the excitement of being at Amherst lay in the challenge of trying to keep track of many issues at once, with almost no one around me paying attention to the way these issues fitted together. The college was a complex organism with many different activities interlocking in different ways, surviving in a complex environment. A given day would bring an immediate urgency, like a black student complaining of unfairness in one of the science departments; a long-term question about how to include new library shelving in a grant application; a discussion of research on desert saints in the patristic period or the genetics of sea urchins; and a conversation about computer networking with another institution. The only thing I could be committed to was the complex whole, with all its ecological interrelationships, and yet the different departments continued to see themselves as competitors. Sometimes I felt as if a whole living planet were turning in my mind, with no one around me willing to share my vision.

The corporate world as it is currently constituted puts a high premium on narrow focus. Only a few people filter through the layers of corporate specialization with a capacity to deal with the multiple issues of a complex organization in its environment. To meet this need, business educators go back, again and again, to the value of the liberal arts and the need to educate generalists. Yet most professors are also narrow, quite incapable of being good deans or presidents because their entire training has been as Johnny one-note. For many, this extends to an inability to teach—if teaching means being attentive to the needs and interests of others. The narrow focus of the industrial organization that gives each assembly-line worker a single bolt to tighten is mirrored in the pressure on executives to attend only to short-term profitability or on researchers to publish in isolated driblets to lengthen their resumes.

But a household requires sustained attention to many different needs, a very different kind of attention. Time, space, and tools need to be used for multiple purposes, leftovers must be varied and combined. Integration becomes more important than specialization. Leftover fabric from a dress will reappear in patchwork five years later; one task may be put aside when the baby wakes up for a different task that allows interaction. Some tasks are undone within minutes, like a cup of tea that is drunk as soon as it is made. Others endure for decades. Getting along with the neighbors and keeping in touch with relatives are part of keeping the house. Why is it that our civilization is so attentive to the economies of scale and blind to the economies of combination?

When Alice talked about the challenges of managing the work of creative people in research and development, it was clear that what she was doing was rescuing them from an excess of multiplicity so that they could concentrate. She carried the integration in her own head. This meant setting aside the technical work she had done with pleasure for years and learning a different kind of creativity that is nearly invisible. "If a project is very complex, someone has to know how to break it down. You have to know how to parcel a problem out in sections in order to have little achievement pieces to give the impetus to go on to the next.

"There are two things about dealing with creative people. One is acknowledging their creativity, exploring it with them, getting them to commit to doing something other than just talking about it, and the other is helping them, because it's a hard process and they can get discouraged, and then you want to be there to talk with them about the latest problem and make them able to go back to it. But the advantage of dealing with creative people is that they really want to finish their creations. They need those little helps when they've lost confidence in what they're doing, and they need to hear from somebody else that they are on track. The thing that keeps them going isn't just charisma—that's what hooks them in—it's achieving. The more one does it, the more one interacts, the quicker one can set up the situation in which they can achieve and recognize that. You can't just walk in when everything is yucked up and say, there there, this is really wonderful. Frequently, when you're exploring some blockage, just doing it is like holding up a mirror, so they can see what they have achieved, and that's more important than the actual advice you give.

"Jack and I were a good team because he always wanted impossible things done, which I always loved. I could see in watching others at what point they got unsure of themselves, so I'd go and talk calmly with them. He would make the impossible demands and then I would break them down in pieces so people wouldn't fall totally apart, and just keep plugging and doing little things to ensure that one would have results. That was very satisfying. In a hi-tech company, new things have to come on-line all the time, a continuous evolution with one product stable while another is changing. I could lose some of my smartest people if they got bored.

"Jack had gotten used to getting quick results, so while I was debugging the initial system, he was driving me crazy because there wasn't anything he could really do except breathe very heavily on the back of my neck. I'd say, here he comes, he's going to breathe again. He was wonderful when there were lots of ideas starting, going around and making sure every pot came to a serious boil. There were lots of things he didn't know anything about, so he had to ask questions, and you couldn't just answer with bullshit. It forced people to think. There was this wonderful period where some of us would be working together and doing experiments, and in the process of explaining to Jack it would become clear where the weaknesses were. That was really good in the area of hardware, but it didn't work in software at all, you don't get a system at the end, just tons and tons of wonderful working pieces that can't be put together. In hardware, pieces can be put together, but in software there has to be top-down design. So our weakest point was software. At the time when that had to be done properly, I was so involved with litigation and raising money that I couldn't pay attention, so we lost a huge amount of time."

One of the striking facts about the women whose lives I have been examining is that the struggle to combine commitments is really a search for ways to make the combinations mutually enhancing. Joan carried her first baby, Kai, with her in a laundry basket to the school where she was teaching in Vienna, to the delight of the children; Johnnetta gave birth in Liberia, learning more about the culture as she interacted with other mothers. When Vanni was born, I joined a research project at MIT analyzing films of mother-infant interaction, knowing that new motherhood would give me a resource of attention and sensitivity. My mother used my early childhood as an opportunity for observation and for testing some of the convictions about childrearing she had developed through her fieldwork. When I wrote about my mother drawing on her experience with me to increase her anthropological understanding, some reviewers were appalled, as if this necessarily entailed a theft of love or its replacement by cold and sterile intellect. In fact, there was a synergy there. Both of us have been better mothers for the inclusion of trained observation in our caring.

Women's lives offer valuable models because of the very pressures that make them seem more difficult. Women have not been permitted to focus on single goals but have tended to live with ambiguity and multiplicity. It's not easy. But the rejection of ambiguity may be a rejection of the complexity of the real world in favor of some dangerously simple competitive model. When a nation goes to war, it no longer has to seek a balance between guns and butter but must give a clear priority to guns; this is why war often comes as such a simplifying relief. Any analytical tool that seems to provide a comparable simplification of the multitude of choices in the real world is embraced—the bottom line, the GNP. Any technique for smoothing diverse values into a single scale, such as the conversion of human lives or clean air into dollars, models this simplification. Women, torn between their own creative energies and concern for each member of their families, are reminded daily that role stereotypes and balance sheets are equally inadequate tools for seeking long-term well-being. These lessons in the arithmetic of caring are available for men as well.

You can't "have it all"—nature doesn't work that way, and finally there are only so many hours in the day. It is, however, almost always possible to have more; having less often means producing less. For Medieval Christians, scholarship and spirituality were considered almost inaccessible without celibacy, but in the Jewish tradition scholarship was associated with virility and sexual potency. The two activities were seen as mutually enhancing rather than competitive. When Alice was denied the engineering scholarship she had earned on test scores, two reasons were given: that she was interested in art and music and literature as well as engineering, and that she was a woman. Both of these facts meant the same thing: that she was insufficiently narrow and would not devote her full capacity to engineering.

My great-grandfather is credited with being one of those who shifted Cambridge University out of its monastic mode so that the fellows of Saint John's College would be permitted to marry, and yet we are struggling still with the notion of competing choices. Perhaps, we worry, men who become truly involved in fatherhood will never produce great achievements in the marketplace. We occasionally honor the possibility that a range of interests might be more fertile than narrow concentration by speaking of Renaissance men of endless vitality and appetite who combine interests in art and science and the increase of wealth with active love lives and large families. But perhaps men and women who are allowed to address multiple commitments in flexible contexts will achieve in new ways. It is not unreasonable to suppose that the kind of synergy we associate with the Renaissance man can develop in the lives of men and women who multiply their spheres of sensitivity and caring.

VICISSITUDES
OF COMMITMENT

ANOTHER KIND OF DIVIDEDNESS haunts our efforts even more than multiple and conflicting commitments—the dividedness created by distrust or doubt. All too often, we find ourselves investing passion and belief in individuals and institutions that cannot be trusted but must instead be approached warily in the face of corruption or potential rejection. The women I have been working with are all idealistic in different ways, committed to abstractions like justice or intimacy and searching for the practical expression of these ideals, but perhaps this is because I came to this project deeply puzzled about the viability of such idealistic commitments in an imperfect world. It is hard enough to put together a graceful composition from diverse components, harder still when the components are shoddy and flawed. Some contradictions cannot be resolved.

I have been especially curious about the relationship between the idealism of dependency, an unquestioning belief in social myths, and idealism as a form of criticism, defining what ought to be even while knowing that it is often not so. It is especially important for women to avoid mistaking the fear of questioning the foundations of their security for commitment. Women have traditionally been vulnerable and have translated vulnerability into a simulacrum of trust. It is possible to be deeply committed to a marriage and still open-eyed, to hedge one's bets against the reality that marriages do come to an end—and then proceed in the belief that careful commitment to a new marriage is still worthwhile. It is also possible to be deeply critical of a person or an institution and still to be committed to it. It may be worthwhile to invest time and resources passionately in support of a cause, but it is wiser to avoid burning bridges or putting on blinkers as the tokens of commitment. A degree of caution need not be equivalent to disloyalty; blindness is not a virtue. My mother once wrote a book about the American national character whose title was drawn from the proverb "Trust in God and keep your powder dry." Women, especially, all too often test the Lord's good will by leaving their gunpowder kegs out in the rain.

The capacity to combine commitment with skepticism is essential to democracy. Since her student days, Johnnetta has taken positions calling for radical change, criticizing what exists. When she became a part of what used to be called "the system," she brought her skepticism with her, reshaped into a building tool. It is not easy to find the right balance between trust and skepticism, commitment and independence. Many people marry again after divorce, but if they have learned from experience the balance will be different.

One of the lines of disillusionment that most people follow is the discovery that parents are less than we as children believed, and this carries over to discoveries about all the structures of authority and institutions in which we work. Oddly enough, as we all know from adolescence, it is possible to question authority passionately, to argue that it is entirely wrongheaded, and still at some level to believe in continuing good will. The real loss is the awareness that good will is absent.

At one level, trust is the premise of a child, a necessity for survival in a position of dependency. Children need to believe in the good will of parents, even when they are neglected or beaten. Often they become convinced that they deserve their sufferings because it is easier to embrace a sense of diffuse guilt and unworthiness than to believe in the malevolence of all-powerful beings. Today, I am unwilling to work from a position of dependent trust, and I believe the capacity to be self-supporting is a precondition to genuine partnership and responsible participation. At the same time, adult trust is a necessity of human social life. When it is violated, it is not easy to build again.

My husband and I went to Iran in 1972 aware, inevitably, that the shah was widely regarded as a corrupt tyrant and that many people were longing for the overthrow of the monarchy. Still, it seemed to us possible to work for improvement within the existing structure, and both Barkev and I looked for openings for constructive change. The Iran Center for Management Studies, where Barkev worked, developed institutional styles for maneuvering within the larger framework. Which member of the royal family would, as a patron, respect the integrity of the institution? How much of a subsidy was it possible to take from the government without losing autonomy? How could one resist pressures to corrupt admissions or hiring without creating antagonism? I had reviewed the work of other social scientists who had characterized Iran as a society built on distrust, so my initial research questions were where to find the kernel of trust that must nevertheless exist for the society to function, and how individuals forged new trust with each other.

Both of us, like our Iranian friends, were ambivalent about the society as it was, even as it was changing in front of our eyes. Corruption was not new to Iran, but in those final years of the monarchy we could see an ancient balance of tolerable corruption becoming unstable. Change was so rapid that it compounded existing abuse, new forms encrusting the old, so that even the cynical were shocked. Gradually, we became aware of an underlying theme in Iranian culture that rejected the ancient arts of compromise and sought absolutes; this theme blossomed under Khomeini's tutelage. In retrospect, however, Iran's earlier patterns of ambiguity and negotiation seem healthier than the burst of blinkered and wasteful euphoria that accompanied the revolution. The Iranian revolution left me with the conviction that moral ambiguity can be a source of strength.

To do research in Iran, I felt it was essential to be a real participant, so I found a variety of jobs in education and educational planning. In 1973 and 1974, I was working in Tehran on the plan for a new university to be built in the city of Hamadan, on the ruins of ancient Ecbatana. Those I was working with were idealists who believed that it would be possible to construct an educational system that would not alienate people from their own culture and set them on the track toward emigration or migration to the capital. The plan, partly modeled after the American land-grant colleges, was to offer regional training in agriculture and education, facilitate the development of health-delivery systems, and help traditional crafts evolve into local industries.

One of the pleasures of my migratory life has been the diversity of institutional types I have worked in, including the University of Hamadan. I have taught in three countries, at large and small institutions, public and private, old and new. I have worked at huge Northeastern University in Boston's center city, founded to train the children of immigrants in nursing and business and engineering; and at tiny Amherst College in a charming small town, offering an intimate version of the liberal arts to the children of privilege. Willy-nilly, many women experience such diversity as part of the discontinuity of their lives. Alice has worked at General Electric and Polaroid, with their totally different corporate cultures, as well as in academic research labs; Ellen has practiced the most privileged kind of individual therapy and has worked in huge state hospitals. Today, Johnnetta is president of Spelman College, which has only 1,600 students; she used to work at the University of Massachusetts at Amherst, which has an enrollment of 25,000. I make choices now out of the habit of enjoying diversity.

At the University of Hamadan, I had been hired to develop a core curriculum in the social sciences. I saw our task as changing the way students looked at familiar patterns and contexts so that they could be both analytical and respectful. They would have to become compassionate observers, pausing to enjoy the perception of patterns that might be enriched or modified, rather than rushing ahead to impose new ones. I was planning on using film and sending students out to do the kinds of fieldwork I have always assigned to my students—interviewing grandparents, learning to look with new eyes at the commonplace.

In Iran at that time, a new university was being established about every two years to absorb the ever increasing numbers of applicants convinced that education was the path to advancement or escape. Bright ideas for different kinds of institutions were batted around the ministries and the court and, like all development projects in Iran, were pulled between the shah's preference for impressive modern developments, hi-tech capital-intensive industries and grandiose constructions, and the concerns of others about more gradual transitions and appropriate technologies.

On the Hamadan project, these two pulls were very obvious. The ministry had assigned the university a site on a hilltop separate from and above the city, perfect for gleaming new buildings insulated from the life of the city, but the architect wanted to build in an old caravanserai in the bazaar, where students would be in constant contact with traditional merchants and artisans. Most serious of all was the fact that the university was really a marriage of two projects developed separately: one was for a populist university, rooted in the traditional sectors; the other was for a Francophone university. At that time, Iran already had several English-language institutions and one emphasizing German, but there was no university based on close current collaboration with France—even though the entire Iranian educational system, with its emphasis on memorization, hierarchy, and competitive examination, with the University of Tehran at the center, had originally been modeled on the French system.

When I had taught earlier at the University of Tehran, I would bring first an American and then an Iranian mother-infant pair into the classroom for observation, to give students a heightened sense of how early and deeply children are shaped to different cultural patterns. As word spread around the campus of this strange event, I could see a succession of eyes pressed to the judas window in the doorway. One year, a member of the class sat ramrod straight and looked out the window for an hour and a half, unable to accept something so trivial as a ten-month-old infant as part of a university lecture. I knew quite clearly, then, the impediments to constructing an educational system on observation rather than authority. Given the historical role of French culture in Iran, collaboration with France was precisely the worse context for this effort. But still, we hoped something would get across.

We were caught in a contradiction, a milder version of the kind of contradiction my father and his colleagues in the study of schizophrenia called a double bind, the requirement that we be both French and not French. The essence of that double bind for me was that I was not supposed to exist. All the Iranians in the project had had a portion of their education in French institutions. Although they were convinced of the inappropriateness of the French model, they could pass as Francophiles. I learned to prefer having my ideas adopted to getting credit for them; I would write informal memoranda that would simply be absorbed into my colleagues' reports for outside circulation. Only once was I publicly included in a gathering of the planning group. I sat demurely opposite Prime Minister Hoveyda at a formal luncheon, as invisible as that infant in the Tehran classroom until the very end, when large and expensive cigars were passed. He suddenly looked straight at me and said, in English, "Of course you won't want one of those."

In the seventies, an Iranian university was attempting to develop a working relationship with Harvard. That relationship was finally declined by Harvard's president, who was quoted to me as saying, "I don't want to lose my virginity on that one." An interesting metaphor. At the simplest level, it was a statement that the collaboration was likely to lead to embarrassment and disillusionment, better to be avoided. At the next level, it could have been an acknowledgment that any such collaboration, like a marriage, would involve a necessary loss of innocence by both parties and the gradual construction of trust in a partner who is never all that one hoped or believed and yet who is someone worth caring about in ways that yesterday one was too simple to imagine. Any collaboration with the shah's Iran was a mixed blessing, but responsible adult participation, like adult sexuality, requires an end to innocence, metaphorical or otherwise, and an acceptance of ambiguity.

There were achievements in those years that still make us feel that our efforts were worthwhile, and odds and ends of our work survive. Some students keep in touch, a few colleagues carry on with a changed sense of what is possible. A portion of our vision for Hamadan survives in the remodeled section of the bazaar, but now it is part of a more radical turning back toward the past. Barkev's institution, the Iran Center for Management Studies, was taken over for the training of revolutionary mullahs. For months when it was being built, I argued for the inclusion of traditional-style toilets that allow religiously correct cleansing, and these have no doubt been constructed. Efforts to incorporate a respect for traditional ways in moving toward modernization were insufficient to overcome the bias of the larger system toward polarization.

The old regime was ridden with moral ambiguity. Today, Iran's leaders seek ideological and religious consistency—and their own power—by looking backward. It is not possible to combine a realistic acceptance of the future with the expectation of consistency; change is inevitably uneven and full of surprises, carrying all the moral uncertainty these changes are likely to entail. The alternative to the fundamentalist call for total reconstruction that produced the present Iranian theocracy was the hope that it would be possible to build within ambiguity, a hope that made it possible for us to work—warily—within the system.

Vanni and I were together on the Caspian in 1978, as the Iranian revolution heated up, and it was easy to become frightened as friends urged us to keep off the streets and try to be invisible. A little girl and her baby brother were killed by a stray bullet as she stood holding him, hidden behind a gate in a nearby village, and I worried that a bereaved father might seek victims for his vengeance. I had Vanni sleeping in my bed and kept a small bag with shoes, passports, and traditional veils, a big one for me and an eight-year-old size for Vanni, beside the back window in case we had to leave in a hurry. But most of the Iranians we had direct contact with were protective. When I had the chance to walk through demonstrations in Tehran, where armored cars of soldiers rolled along the avenues firing tear-gas canisters up on the rooftops, strangers would draw me into sheltered doorways and would respond warmly when I spoke to them in Persian. Barkev and I lost a great deal in the Iranian revolution, years of work and cherished possessions, and had to start again like refugees. We were spared memories of personal hostility and betrayal, but it was the end of a chapter in our lives.

Johnnetta commented to me on her innocence when she went off to college, but black children learn early that the good guys don't always win, and disenchantment had begun for her with the discovery of the bigotry waiting for black children beyond their front doors. After that, she went through a series of disillusionments that have ultimately been empowering and brought her to the point of being an effective critic and reformer, far more moderate and realistic than she once was. The discovery that the first man she loved was addicted to heroin was a disillusionment with a curious core of reassurance, the decency of her potential father-in-law, who refused to let her waste her life and vitality on the conviction that a good wife could be the young man's salvation. Of all the women I worked with, Johnnetta has been the most ideologically committed. She had had to work toward an understanding of the flaws and blind spots in those with whom she shared passionate convictions in the civil-rights movement, in postrevolutionary Cuba, and at the University of Massachusetts. The fact that a cause is right is no guarantee of fairness and decency in the people that espouse it or benefit from it. The very people who are most committed to some significant frontier of social justice or compassion are likely to become locked in self-serving battles for dominance. The corruption of progressive hope in Maurice Bishop's Grenada into dogmatism and internal conflict and the resultant takeover and assassination probably marked the end of Johnnetta's early idealism. Anyone who has been involved in trying to support and encourage outsiders to move into full participation knows something about disillusionment. All too often, the noble disinherited and their advocates prove to be fractious and inept, or even vicious and corrupt.

Each of us has repeatedly had to salvage a capacity for commitment as we became aware of the flaws of institutions and indeed of the individuals who seemed to embody those commitments. Like all the other discontinuities we have faced, this implies possibility as well as loss, the need to construct a new mode of self-preservation, and, finally, commitment without dependency.

At Amherst, as in Iran, I worked for gradual change within a system that I knew was flawed, but I did not work warily enough. Ambiguity is perhaps easier to endure when you are a visitor, an outsider who has her own place to return to. One of the costs of living abroad, for me, was that I remained unduly hopeful about my own society, expecting to feel at home, but Amherst was still caught in the set of inherited attitudes that defined any woman as an outsider. My optimism, which survived the Iranian revolution, was shattered by my experiences there, but today I find myself believing once again that it is worthwhile to try to work gradually within an imperfect system, to look for ways in which values already embedded in it, however ambiguously, can find fuller expression.

I experienced Amherst at its worst, partly by accident and partly because the ordinary and partial decencies of the system failed to function for a woman. My initial honeymoon on that gracious campus had been followed by a dip and a reappraisal. I had overcome the initial obstacles and felt happy and confident, with a sufficient mix of criticism and hope. I had a wealth of growing friendships and a sense, after two and a half years with only minor crises, of broad faculty respect and support. Then in January 1983, I rolled my car on an icy road in New Hampshire. I was not significantly injured, but within the same twenty-four hours Julian Gibbs, the Amherst president, died suddenly, and my entire experience was turned around.

There were certain things that were crystal clear to me immediately—too clear, for one of the effects of shock is a certain spurious simplification. The immediate formal responsibility for the college in the president's absence lies with the dean of the faculty; the college had, in fact, always tended to function more smoothly when he was away. I decided that I would not want to be a candidate for the Amherst presidency when a new search was mounted. I would conceal my accident and devote myself to ensuring calm and continuity, with the illusory clarity that comes from having laid self-interest aside. I ignored my bruises and the steady ache in my neck and worked around the clock, exactly as I would have concealed a headache if Vanni had come to me in some distress.

The chairman of the board arrived in a near panic and pressed me to agree to accept the acting presidency during the interim. Worried about precedents in which women are said to have declined responsibility, I reluctantly said that I would do it. Then in a flurry of conflicting advice, I gradually became intrigued by the possibility of doing well, on a temporary basis, the tasks I had seen done badly. Under the pressure of emergency arrangements, I didn't really grieve for Julian until the college memorial service, but when the chaplain reached the phrase, "and light perpetual shine upon them," I suddenly saw Julian's face turned up to the sun, boyish and free as it must have been on his sailboat, away from the administrative tasks he hated, and started sobbing helplessly. The portrait that hangs now in Johnson Chapel, with the array of other men who have been presidents of Amherst, captures exactly that look and makes me want to weep for this sweet willful man who was such a poor president and was so easy to mother.

The six-person executive committee of the faculty normally meets with the president as chairperson and the dean as recording secretary. Because I felt that I had a conflict of interest, I suggested that the group meet without me, before meeting with the board. I was probably more trusting than normal because I was grieving and in shock, a state in which one hopes for friendship and reaches out for shared values and commitments. Then too, if you work all day in your garden, you can forget that your neighbor may covet it as real estate. In the event, a majority of the Committee of Six advised the board of trustees against making me acting president. Several of their own number, they noted, would be "more reassuring" to the faculty in that role. It was only weeks later that I began, like a good detective, to ask, not *cherchez la femme,* but *cui bono,* who benefits?

In any long-term community, there is a certain check on the crudest forms of self-interest because the wise know that everyone benefits from continuity and cooperation. But there is always a tendency to grab when a chance comes along—perhaps as a result of an emergency—to divide up the pie. Some people rescue survivors after a natural disaster; others turn to looting.

In places like Amherst some grow to feel that the institution is their personal property, so they are more concerned with whether their writ runs than with outcomes. There was an odd mirroring between the distortions in my vision and those of a handful of senior men, equally caused by identification with the institution. I tended to identify my interests with those of the college; they identified the interests of the college with their own. The same kind of complementary distortion often happens in marriage. Women are taught to deny themselves for the sake of the marriage, men are taught that the marriage exists to support them.

It took several months for me to unravel the sequence of events. Later that spring, I wrote, still indignant, "What hurt most was having my trust betrayed by the Committee of Six. It sounds crazy because you've heard me complain about them, the hours and hours of meetings, week after week, but . . . some of the stuff that comes through my office is so scuzzy that I really began to rely on C6 to keep me believing in this place. At its best, it represents a sort of distilled aspiration for fairness and clarity. But that was when we were in there with them. When the committee met alone, it bypassed its basic responsibility of advising me—after all, I was the acting administration—and it just ignored its normal standards about gossip and unattributed reports. And they're not dumb. See, they didn't have to denounce me, just to express *concern*—there are alums on that board who aren't even used to coeducation yet."

The board, convened in an all-male emergency quorum, ratified the coup. They argued in secret all afternoon, and then made Armour Craig, the senior member of the committee and an alumnus of the college, acting president. A graceful man and a dedicated teacher who had never held an administrative position where he had to make unpopular decisions, Armour told me later that his first thought when he heard of Julian's death was that perhaps, in the last year before his retirement, he would be made acting president of his alma mater. So unembarrassed was he that his first reaction to Julian's death was one of personal ambition, that he has made me wonder whether the impulse to service was somehow perverse, like Johnnetta's long ago willingness to sacrifice her life to marriage to a drug abuser. When I heard rumors, after Armour had been a year in office, that, much to his surprise and distress, he had been hung in effigy by students demonstrating against the abolition of fraternities, I was struck by the irony that perhaps only now was he learning that an administration behaving appropriately and responsibly still runs risks of unpopularity.

It was a grim spring for me. You cannot keep someone in a position of trust and responsibility when it is obvious that you are lying to them and publicly denying them confidence. My own continuing sense of responsibility kept me from any public complaint. Key people offered me support after the fact, but the bullying and gentlemanly shunning that some of the powerful men on the faculty had always practiced were redoubled, for they had been reconfirmed in their traditional oligarchy by the board. My neck went on hurting, like a nagging form of survivor guilt, and unconsciously I think I felt I was being punished because it was Julian who had died in that terrible twenty-four-hour period, and I, who had spent so much time protecting him and protecting the college from him, should have died in his place.

When a new president was chosen, he came to the quick and obvious conclusion while still in New York and asked for my resignation, citing a curiously distorted catalog of second-hand complaints. Only a dean who had done a very bad job would have been treated as I was treated, he said, unless it was a matter of sexism, and he had been assured that there was no sexism at Amherst. The deanship was given to another member of the Committee of Six. Thus the college bypassed affirmative-action hiring procedures for the very person obliged to enforce them. There was a good deal of faculty concern about the propriety of these decisions, but there is also a widespread feeling at Amherst that long-term faculty members are governed by different rules than newcomers.

There are many reasons for the maintenance of such double standards. The classical double standard says that men may violate the public rules of sexual behavior with impunity and women may not; in a wider sense, a double standard is any rule that controls the behavior of those without power while permitting another group to flout those rules, further enhancing their own power, whether by images of sexual potency or the wealth resulting from insider trading. Some Americans believe that the president of the United States is bound by the laws and the Constitution. Others, including two presidents, seem to believe he is not. We have been going through a period of transition for about twenty years, struggling to become a nation with one law for weak and strong alike; this means tightened scrutiny of the powerful, the introduction of vast numbers of clumsy procedural codes, and legal challenges intended to achieve equity. We have to be flexible about the codes and understanding of the problems of readjustment, but we can go only so far in "grandfathering" patriarchy and discrimination.

As in Iran, corruption is a by-product of the ambiguity produced by change. Such corruption often involves people who regard themselves as upright; the behaviors they take for granted are relabeled by changing moral standards and they fail to learn new ways. One college professor, who had been praised for his willingness to work with fraternities and his avuncular "boys will be boys" attitude, went on meeting with the fraternities in secret after they had been abolished, virtue transmuted into subversion. During Prohibition, many

Americans found familiar behavior suddenly outside the law and became scofflaws in the effort to maintain old habits. But this process undermined other kinds of law-abiding behavior and created a new criminal class. Both the Mafia and the Ku Klux Klan grew from assertions of local autonomy against rules perceived as alien. Now they are criminal. At one time, most decisions in society were made informally by highly placed male elders; the old-boy network was the legitimate way of doing business. Today, that behavior is no longer acceptable, but responsible elders may be tempted to continue old styles of behavior in secret, turning themselves into conspirators. Men who feel that their income or authority has been wrongly eroded may rationalize furtive moonlighting or sift minority applicants out of a pool without seeing themselves as thieves or bigots. Change is hard on everyone—hard on those who have to adjust, hard on those in positions of responsibility who seem to be taking away traditional privileges.

When I was a child, I often heard complaints about the exclusion of Jews, and Jews were often accused of having a persecution complex. But in America today, the complaint has become less common and Jews have far more complete participation in society. Some complaints of racism and sexism may also be exaggerated, but when racism and sexism are really gone, the complaints will also fade away. One of the problems that complicates talking about these matters is that no active dislike is needed for one group to wish to hold on to privilege at the expense of another group, felt to be outsiders. Nowadays, prejudice is relative, not absolute. There is no fixed rule that excludes, just a different probability, a slight stacking of the cards against certain people, a different and more destructive standard of judgment that makes every error fatal. It's like going to a gambling casino: if you know that all the games are rigged to guarantee a certain profit to the house, you also know that if you play long enough you will lose everything, even if the house edge is only a few percent. We live in a world in which many positions are open to women, but there is always that slight stacking of the deck, the extra stress, the waiting prejudice that amplifies every problem.

It took me a long time to recover from my experience at Amherst, going over it again and again, working out what had happened and why. It was important to me to analyze the institution's patterns as well as to review my own mistakes. It was also interesting to realize that traditional gender patterns played a role not only in the bias of others but also in my habitual reluctance to complain. I had repeatedly accepted inappropriate burdens, stepping in to do what needed to be done. In retrospect, I think I carried them well, but the cost was that I was chronically overloaded, weary, and short of time for politicking, smoothing ruffled feathers, and simply resting. Watching the priorities of the new administration was educational. If an institution is lucky, it gets a few drops of vision and integrity mixed in with the politics. It has always struck me that for all his lack of integrity Nixon seemed to be an effective president until he got caught.

Anger was an achievement, a step away from the chasm of despair. Women in this society tend to be disproportionally damaged by such experiences, because we are too ready to accuse ourselves of failure and too reluctant to surrender trust once it is granted, whether to a spouse or an institution. Often, American men learn to project their disappointments outward, like Lee Iacocca using his rejection by Ford to fuel new achievements; women tend to internalize their losses. When a proposal is turned down or a job not offered, women tend to say, I wasn't worthy. Men more often contend that the process was crooked.

I taught at Amherst for another year and a half after Julian's death and considered remaining there, because I found myself so rich in friendships, perhaps more and more diverse than at any other time in my life. But the faculty at small colleges, because of their isolation, become especially dependent on the institution. It was frustrating to watch those who felt battered or threatened by the new administration and to be unable to help. There had been only a single grievance petition presented in the three years that I was dean; now there were so many that the college established a new committee to review them.

I wrote to the president when I resigned, after going on unpaid leave, "Over the past three years, I have experimented with a number of possible ways of remaining affiliated to the college and continuing to use my influence for improvement. This is because when I came to Amherst I was making what I believed to be a permanent commitment, and it was in the nature of my job that I cultivated an admiration for the institution that has only been relinquished with reluctance. . . . The question for me has been one of trust. Returning to the institutional dependency of teaching on a two-semester basis would have required a degree of trust and commitment I can no longer muster."

Amherst is a curious place. All that confidence of virtue based on past donations for the training of poor youths for the ministry, now supplemented by tuitions in five figures to train corporate lawyers and stockbrokers. All those worldly and successful executives on the board, who let nostalgia for their undergraduate days cloud their perceptions of the present. A faculty of high intelligence and considerable integrity cocooned in complacent myths. It is easy for an institution like Amherst College to live on its capital, but the capital that is slowly being spent is not the endowment—that continues to grow, for wealth attracts wealth—but the institution's moral capital of trust and good will and reputation.

Finally, the question is not about what was done to me or what has been done to other women. Many institutions celebrate the transition to integration by a series of human sacrifices, so that only the second or third woman in a given role has a chance of survival. After that, things slowly improve. The issue is that society supports the privileges of places like Amherst in the belief that educational institutions contribute to a consensus that involves both openness and continuity, intellectual skepticism and moral commitment. They will not do this without criticism.

I see the women I have worked with on this project pouring their energies into their work, and I know that the society benefits, but I puzzle about whether they should cultivate cynicism and disengagement rather than risk trusting those who are not trustworthy. The new president of Amherst told me once, when he was toughing out the faculty protests at the end of his first year (with board support), that he "keeps his bags packed." It may be that he had learned from my experience, but it was the wrong lesson. In retrospect, I don't wish that I had kept my bags packed. The phrase is current in many parts of corporate America, where some companies treat executives as replaceable pawns to be moved from place to place. Only a few value loyalty and understand that it can be cultivated only where it is reciprocated. Commitment is elusive without trust, and yet the double standard itself creates a double bind as the trust and idealism of those who cannot defend themselves are used to force their collusion in dishonesty.

We draw on the experiences of others and understand them better in the process. Jack had been dispossessed at Orion only a year before my problems at Amherst, so I had the examples of his desperate search for redress and Alice's conviction that creative work would be the only real solution. I know women who have invested their emotional and financial resources in lawsuits and have been permanently crippled as a result. I have followed hostile divorces that began in betrayal and left women with impossible economic burdens and lasting bitterness. I don't believe it is healthy to live, as some foreign wives did in Iran, with your metaphorical bags packed, but I have come to believe that when the end comes it pays to cut your losses, for there is almost always more ahead than we can guess.

Of the women I worked with, Ellen is probably the most resiliently aware of the lack of integrity in the systems with which she has to deal. She has been very clear about her reluctance to again be a part of a large rigid institution, yet she is strongly committed. At the beginning of our friendship, when I was still aching from the Amherst experience, she was turned down for a grant. Instead of feeling personal rejection, she was ready to analyze the politics. She is deeply committed as a therapist, but she looks at her medical colleagues with a sharper eye than most physicians—for if any group protect their own claims of virtue more fiercely than professors, it is physicians.

When Ellen talked about her decision to resign from her job as director of the emergency psychiatric service at Beth Israel Hospital, she described the difficulties of being enmeshed in the giving of inadequate or ineffective care, and the ways in which the multiplication of regulations and litigation, originally designed to improve care, makes caregiving more difficult. "Emergency rooms all over the country were coming under the gun at the point that I quit. That kind of patient care is filled with enormous frustration. You ended up participating in the dumping of patients from the poorest groups, who really needed care, and it got worse every year. We had a little revolving door between our facility and the Massachusetts Mental Health Center at the state hospital two and a half blocks away, the so-called last resort facility. We'd get the patients, and send them down the street, and then *they* wouldn't admit them because their threshold for illness was far higher, because they were deluged, and they'd send them back. You'd often do it by ambulance, because you had to be sure nothing happened to the patient in between. And it wasn't our fault, and it wasn't their fault. It was just that you were caught in this insane system.

"A large element of what I had to do as head of the emergency ward was deflecting the fire from that kind of really terrible patient care, a real kind of dumping and so-called referral of patients to places we knew they wouldn't be allowed to stay. It was something that I think was very hard for all of us, that we couldn't help. You know, your hands were tied. Resources were just not there. I remember many times speaking to hospital lawyers saying, 'What do we do? We can't just kick this patient out. There's no place for him to go,' and being told, 'Just be sure you document everything.' ''

I could compare my frustrations at Amherst College with Johnnetta's at U. Mass. and realize that the college was not really more corrupt than hundreds of other institutions. I learned for the first time, when I started this book, the details of Alice's efforts to sustain her company through a no-win legal battle and the sexism of the Boston financial community. Joan told me what it felt like in Berkeley when one friend after another capitulated to McCarthyite pressure to sign a loyalty oath while the Eriksons, with more immediate memories of prewar Europe, held out—and how one after another, their shamefaced friends began to avoid them. I could begin to sort out the need to live in an imperfect world from the need to maintain a vision of a better one.

"If you are going to be in the business world, there are lots of rules that you may not agree about as a human being," Alice said, "but they are there and you have to observe them without compromising your own values or saying they shouldn't be there. If you are going to war you have a certain obligation to win and not let everyone who is following you be destroyed. If you adopt profitability as a criterion, it is not a necessity to be a bastard. But in crisis mode things get out of hand. You can't have expectations of the other party. You can wish for them but you have to act on observations of reality as it really is."

Nevertheless, when there is a rent in the canvas, a discord in the harmony, a betrayal, it is important not only to recover but to discover a new and inclusive pattern of meaning. Part of the task of composing a life is the artist's need to find a way to take what is simply ugly and, instead of trying to deny it, to use it in the broader design. There is a famous story about a Chinese master painting a landscape. Just as he is nearly finished, a drop of ink falls on the white scroll, and the disciples standing around him gasp, believing the scroll is ruined. Without hesitating, the master takes the finest of hair brushes and, using the tiny globe of ink already fallen, paints a fly hovering in the foreground of the landscape. For a large and wealthy institution, criticism is like the buzzing of a fly, but the purpose here is to discover grace and meaning in a picture larger still.

FITS AND STARTS

As a college student, I read Erik Erikson's book on the life cycle, *Childhood and Society,* and then his second book, on Martin Luther. Like every other student encountering those works, I asked myself how I was doing in resolving my own identity crisis. I had spent my senior year of high school in Israel and had come back to the United States to start college with a deep sense of dividedness, of having first found a new sense of myself in Israel and then having left that clarity behind. The new task was to combine and translate, to put an American gentile identity together with my Israeli experience and to use my college education to shape them into some new whole.

Like many people, I understood Erik's concept of identity as single, something ideally achieved once and enduring for a lifetime, although sometimes deferred or incomplete. But in recent years, he and Joan have increasingly emphasized that although certain crises—moments of opportunity and danger—are focused at particular points in the life cycle, each is prefigured in earlier experience, and each must be addressed again and again. Joan described her conviction that she could be a dancer in the classic language of their early work, as a moment of knowing that she had become most fully herself. But her life is the story of shaping other meaningful commitments from that early certainty, of improvising and piecing together. Each of us has repeatedly had to pose the question of who we are.

Women are accustomed to tasks that have to be done again and again, tasks undone almost as soon as they are done. The dinner is eaten right after it is cooked, and there will be another dinner to think about tomorrow; the bed is unmade every night. But most work is repetitive even if one is not making the same bed or washing the same dishes. Still, there are skills that improve and tasks that stay done, if not forever then for a long time, like building a new roof or planting a tree. There is a special satisfaction to repetitive tasks that have an underlying, barely perceptible rhythm of change, such as washing and folding blue jeans that grow gradually larger over the course of a childhood, or preparing a dish that has been served over and over that suddenly provides the setting for newly mature conversation. Of Johnnetta's three sons, Aaron, her second son, had the hardest time with her divorce and the move to New York, which took him out of his high school just before his senior year. Then when he moved on to become a student at NYU, the evenings in their Brooklyn apartment had a completely new quality. "He is just one righteous kid to be around now. Those two years in New York with Aaron at NYU were such fun for me, both of us working late at night and writing, and he'd want to talk through a paper. Not that we're colleagues, but that he encouraged a kind of mentoring that I have really enjoyed."

The same kind of spiral underlies the shaping and reshaping of identity, as gradually we have more to work with and we become skilled in reconstruction. I ask myself what I would do if my life hit another deep chasm of discontinuity like the Iranian revolution or a move to another country. Even as I reject the idea, I realize that now I know how to pack my bags and how to unpack them, how to discover myself as a part of a new community.

Composing a life is a little like making a Middle Eastern pastry, in which the butter must be layered in by repeated folding, or like making a samurai sword, whose layers of differently tempered metal are folded over and over. As a young college student, Joan knew with certainty that she was a dancer. Over time, this identity has meant being a teacher and a therapist, a wife and a mother, a craftswoman and a writer. From the vantage point of a seventeen year old, this would have looked like a jumble; seen now, from her eighties, it makes sense.

In traditional societies, the transitions in the life cycle come more easily, for the fundamental recognition of one's place in the social fabric dictates them. In our society, these transitions are more painful. College students feel under pressure to make the right career choices quickly, to get onto a track and stay on it, but life shifts constantly. When paths disappear in the underbrush or are blocked, we face the problem of finding a new path that will seem like a continuation of the old.

Joan's life has two patterns of discontinuity woven through it: the familiar discontinuities of women's life cycle, bearing and raising three children, and the discontinuities of Erik's career, involving constant reconstructions of her own. When Joan and Erik married, the practical side of life was more difficult than it has been for any of the rest of us, however much we had to scrimp and save as newlyweds. Erik and Joan set up housekeeping in a tiny house, "like a peanut," outside Vienna, far from the road. The only indoor plumbing was a pump in the kitchen that froze in the winter; so they had to bring water from outside. When Joan was pregnant she had the bad luck to find an indifferent and careless doctor, and Erik was sick when Kai was born in 1931 and then again when Jon was born in 1933. "Talk about couvade!" Joan said. "Erik always did it, though he couldn't get anyone to minister to him."

Most discussions of the improvement in the status of women emphasize increasing rights and increasing conveniences. It is easy to forget how much safer childhood is than it used to be, and that this is a major liberating factor. We all worry when a child is sick, but the ordinary infectious diseases of childhood look very different in the age of antibiotics. Joan's story is punctuated with tales of illness.

"We had had a bad time in New Haven. The boys had both had chicken pox, and Jon had mastoid problems and needed surgery. Then, when Erik went to live with the Sioux, Kai got scarlet fever, and the two boys had to be isolated, one upstairs and one down, for six weeks. So that's what I did while Erik was with the Sioux." Erik's trip was one of the first great efforts to examine psychoanalytic insights across cultural differences; Joan stayed at home. The following year, Jon had more mastoid problems, and they tried him out on sulfa and gave him an overdose. Joan was pregnant, running back and forth between Kai and Jon and feeling torn about leaving Jon in the hospital. He was pulled through with a transfusion given by Joan's sister, but he was sick for a long time. "He needed somebody's undivided attention, but he didn't get it. I always felt badly about that. And then Sue arrived, and along came the decision to move to California. It would have been better if we had stayed another year on the East Coast and given a chance for Jon to recover and for me to look after Sue. It's hard to balance between a newcomer and an older child that needs extra attention and is whiney and doesn't evoke maternal instincts in the same way as a baby.

"Sue's arrival was an interesting event. First Kai and then Jon got mumps, and then I got it and swelled up like a toad. Just when I was through with the swelling, Sue decided to arrive, and since I was still in quarantine, they put me at the end of the contagious ward, but they couldn't decide what to do with Sue. The pains stopped and started again, it was late at night and no attendant was available. Along came Erik in a white jacket, so he decided he would have to deliver, but then he sounded the alarm, and the docs all congregated in the hall discussing where to put the baby.

I said, you're not going to take this baby away. Since they couldn't think of anything better to do they let me keep her. I had such a ball. Having a girl was kind of necessary with two boys. Great fun to be so intimate with the other sex as it were, really getting to know something he-male, but now I had the daughter I had longed for. So that was the start of rooming-in in New Haven Hospital."

Joan was whimsical about the problems of settling in California. "On the first day the boys went to school, I had sent them in knickerbockers. They were furious: 'Nobody wears things like this!' So I had to get them somehow into jeans for the next day. Then they went scouting off to see the town and got lost and had to ask their way. Finally they asked a policeman—they knew the address but not how to find it—so he brought them back and said, 'You better teach these kids their phone number.' 'I didn't get it done yesterday,' I said, 'but by tomorrow I'll get it clear.' "

The first major uprooting had occurred when the Eriksons decided in 1933, with the approach of the Nazi danger, to leave Austria. They quickly discovered that resettling in Denmark, where Erik had been born, would be almost impossible because Erik had been adopted by his German stepfather. Later, when they were in the United States (first in Connecticut and then in California) and war began, Erik was classified as a refugee scholar, but Canadian-born Joan was startled to find herself classified as an enemy alien because she had married a German citizen.

The United States no longer lets such changes of legal status override birth without personal choice, but many countries still do; changes at one level involve the threat of changes at other levels, redefinitions of identity. When I was interviewing the foreign wives of Iranians, I found that for many of them, their cultural problems were overshadowed by the fact that in marrying an Iranian they had automatically become subjects of the shah. Marriage literally determined identity. The United States did not deny their citizenship, but they could no longer use American passports to leave Iran and could only leave with Iranian passports, which required their husbands' permission. In the same way, regardless of conviction, their marriages technically made them Muslims and subject to Muslim laws of marriage, divorce, and inheritance.

A second political move came in 1951, an echo of the first as Joan and Erik withdrew once again from a changing political atmosphere. They had of course both taken oaths of loyalty to the United States when they were granted citizenship, but as Joseph McCarthy's waves of red-baiting increased, the University of California started to require annual loyalty oaths from all faculty. Erik first refused to sign. Then, seeing friends pressured into signing, even though the university was unwilling actually to dismiss him, he resigned. The family moved back East.

Each of these moves, as well as four or five less painful moves over the years, meant that Joan first had to concentrate on reestablishing home life and then look again for her own distinctive niche. Joan was what used to be called "just a housewife" from about 1933 to 1948. In fact, she was also busy in those years organizing activities in the arts for her children. In doing so, she was laying the groundwork for a theory of the relationship between artistic and sensory learning on the one hand, and development and healing on the other. She was also collaborating on all of Erik's work, so that in 1950 when the work on the life cycle was presented at a conference, it bore her name along with Erik's. It was not until 1948 that Joan started to learn jewelry making, finding the space and time for a new art after an apparent fifteen-year hiatus. The forging of a sense of identity is never finished. Instead, it feels like catching one's image reflected in a mirror next to a carousel—"Here I am again." Johnnetta, describing the experience of returning to work at a black college in the South, quoted Malcolm X: "What go round come round."

Almost everyone faces discontinuities that take as long to recover from as a distant move, for almost all of us must deal with the deaths of our parents. A year is the magic time period that is often given for recovery from bereavement—longer than allowed by the forms of our society, shorter than the customs that expect widows to mourn forever. I heard that estimate from a friend who was given it by a psychiatrist after his father's death. He found it immensely helpful, liberating him from stereotypes of masculine imperturbability, but I no longer remember when he passed it on to me. Was it after the death of my first child very soon after his birth in Manila in 1968, or ten years later after my mother died, or was it after some other loss or interruption? I've heard the same recovery period applied to a disastrous fire in which a home is destroyed, the traumatic loss of a job, an amputation.

For an adult with an independent adult life, the loss of a parent carries all the weight of childhood attachment, but at least the texture of everyday life is unbroken. For a man or woman with an independent work life, the loss of a spouse still permits continuity in half the day. Often we lose a part of life because of what we choose to retain, leaving either a home or a career to retain the other.

When Jack died suddenly, he had just emerged from the shadow of a series of losses. He had lost the company he had spent the previous twenty years building, had left a home and ended a marriage; his death came only a few days after he became reassured that the new company he had started with Alice and the house he had bought would not slip away. Because everything was still so much in flux, he had not formalized his divorce or written a new will. Alice found herself living in a house to which she had no claim, trying to hold together the company she and Jack had built, in which she had only the token holdings needed to make her a legal director, but not enough to give her control.

Jean and Alice stood together in the immediate aftermath of Jack's death, but as the weeks passed and both of them encountered different advice and pressures, Alice acted to retain her role as de facto leader of Demonics, as the only way to maintain the company's tenuous momentum so that the effort already invested would result in a viable product. Jean brought lawsuits against Alice and the company—as if the equity Jean now owned would have any value without some maintenance of continuity. Alice moved to her North End condo and traveled back and forth between Japan and her research program, lifting her spirits by studying written and spoken Japanese, enduring the horrors of endless legal sessions. We kept hoping that if the two women could deal with each other directly, they would understand that unless they worked together they would both lose, but the pressures toward adversarial solutions were too great. Ultimately, Jean settled for a portion of what she had wanted, and Alice became a major stockholder and remained chief executive. Unfortunately, she had been forced to squander half of her time and vitality for a full year that could have been used to make the company more viable. The two women had planned Jack's funeral together, but when a stone was erected on Jack's grave a year later, there were two different ceremonies an hour apart, although many of us stolidly stayed for both.

Alice changed the name of Demonics to Rise Technology and took it public in 1987. A year later, after major internal conflicts about marketing, she had moved back to directing research, a new CEO was in place, and she was preparing to move on. But in the course of that year, she had discovered whole new dimensions of herself, a willingness to take responsibility and exercise leadership and a fascination with Japanese culture. Suddenly her concern for aesthetics, which had seemed to pull against her work as an engineer, began to make a valuable contribution to her work.

Why is it that losses so often cluster? My mother died in 1978; within two months, I had lost a job and a home to the Iranian revolution. It took a year to deal with the complexities of closing my mother's office; then, in 1980, just before I began a new job, my father died. I tried to meet the resulting obligations with my left hand and set aside the emotions of transition while I tried to administer Amherst with my right. When Julian Gibbs died in January 1983 and my job fell apart, it felt like more of the same.

Every loss recapitulates earlier losses, but every affirmation of identity echoes earlier moments of clarity. In the aftermath of Julian's death and the betrayal that followed, I wrote a memoir of my parents that at least completed my grieving for them, working through their deaths and through much that was incomplete or unspoken between us. Reviewers remarked that the book had an elegiac tone, without knowing how much I struggled to project the light of my childhood through the shadows of recent months. But when I finished, I was able to say, I am a writer, just as Joan could affirm that she is a dancer.

New beginnings don't happen overnight. I didn't resign from Amherst in the heat of the moment; I took my time in leaving, returning to teach for a year and a half after the new administration was in place. I watched the discontents and turbulence of that first year and became increasingly proud of my own work and freed from the desire to think well of the institution.

I think I brought Amherst to a turning point in its treatment of women. At the end of my last year in the dean's office, I set up a minimum agenda to address the problem of sexism, which was eventually adopted in its entirety by the board. The first step in the agenda was to create several positions for senior women so that Amherst would not constantly be isolating and rejecting vulnerable young women of talent and so that there could be a critical mass of women faculty, for young teachers need secure role models as much as students do. The agenda also included the appointment of additional women to the board and the abolition of fraternities. That spring, I finally found a statistical key to demonstrating at least one aspect of the exploitation of women on the faculty. This finding led to the formation of an investigatory committee, which wrote eloquently about the ways in which women had been placed in contradictory situations and their "lives made unnecessarily and unduly difficult." Today, Amherst is a better place for women faculty and students.

When I left, it was to take a leave without pay to experiment with a writing career, until I found a combination of teaching and writing that would make sense at George Mason University. The identity of a writer is a frightening one—you know that you must work in solitude, without a clear defining context and without a reassuring response for months at a time. The prospect daunted me in high school, but the identity of writer remains truest to my sense of self. Given that I am a writer, as Joan is a dancer, I have put on other roles: linguist and anthropologist, educational planner and academic dean, and always, as part of my nurturing, teacher and lecturer. Writing is the most portable form of creativity, sometimes a vocation and sometimes an avocation. Each time some other engagement has been interrupted, I have gone back to clean paper. Otherwise I would probably be trapped today in narrow expertise, working in some prestigious and arid university department. Writing has been the constancy through which I have reinvented myself after every uprooting.

Often continuity is visible only in retrospect. When this project started, Ellen expected to work out of her home indefinitely, but in 1988 she became president of a new organization called the Better Homes Foundation, created to raise money and fund demonstration projects to help homeless families. "This year has been an incredible culmination of a transition that started at the Bunting five years ago. There's a process that occurs that you don't even know is going on, but with my interests this is the opportunity of my life work-wise. I made a decision not to be institutionally affiliated, because being in an institution means you can't run your own life. But this is an organization I'm building myself, with people that have the same belief systems—wonderful people—and I'm going to run this thing, which is like a dream come true. I don't know how successful we're going to be, but at the minimum we'll be able to operate as a technical-assistance group. I always had the fantasy as a little kid that I wanted to be effective in some way, to be able to change things. It's very exciting. We have the opportunity to make this grow together. It makes me feel as if I'm free. I feel grounded but also disoriented." Ellen laughed, looking ruefully at her blue jeans and the dog at her feet. "It's a new work life that I've created. I'll have to get some clothes—and what about Suzie, she'll have a nervous breakdown!"

When Johnnetta's husband left Amherst, accompanied by the new woman in his life, Johnnetta was working as associate provost at U. Mass., trying to develop a new general-education program that would be adopted by the university faculty. It wasn't. Furthermore, the provost she had worked with, one of her principal mentors and intellectual colleagues, was shortly thereafter rejected by the committee searching for a new chancellor. He subsequently resigned from the administration and returned to teaching. Like me, Johnnetta found herself no longer at home where she had lived and worked, in her case for twelve years. But she moved out slowly, first returning to teaching at U. Mass., then taking a year's leave and renting her house while she went to teach at Hunter College in New York, and finally resigning from U. Mass. Hunter felt good.

When the call came to become president of Spelman College, it felt even better. Johnnetta described her arrival at Spelman at age fifty in the same language of tentative and then joyous self-recognition that Joan had used in speaking of herself as a dancer. We were sitting looking out of a bedroom window in Reynolds Cottage, and the bells began to ring in Sisters' Chapel next door, whose name refers to two white sisters, in whose honor it was donated, but echoes today with the significance of sisterhood to black women. "Those bells go deep inside of me," Johnnetta said. Then she grinned, intoning, "and on the stroke of eight. . . ." She paused.

"On the stroke of eight," I said, throwing away my intention to start the interview with childhood memories, "I want you to start talking about what it feels like to be here now as president of this place, and how it fits into your life."

"I have a ritual that I may cease to participate in," she answered slowly, "but I need that ritual right now. When I awaken in the morning, before I leave my bed, I tell myself again that I am the president of Spelman College. I need that ritual for several reasons. One is that I haven't spent a great deal of my time imagining myself in this sort of a place, in a presidency, so that my image of myself really was not as a college president. My image of myself was to do things beyond being a professor, sure, but it didn't have much reality to it. Now I'm going very quickly through imagining and being. So every morning I have to wake up and tell myself that I'm the president of Spelman College, and then I have to understand again what kind of institution this is.

"On the other hand, the first few days have gone . . . I'm tempted to use that word that any anthropologist ought to be suspicious of—it feels so 'natural.' There's a passage in one of Andrew Salkey's poems, a woman in Cuba telling her kin in Jamaica that life is tough but things are getting better, and then she ends by saying, 'but you know, I feel more like my natural self.' An element of that is seeing myself mirrored in Spelman. One is always mirrored, but here that process is especially meaningful. Spelman is an institution for black women, so this mirroring is really quite literal. And all the tools of our trade, of anthropology, are part of it too. This place is absolutely overflowing with history. You just can't be here without encountering what so much of black America is about. So there's the mirroring of self that is part of falling in love, and also that particular juncture of passion and intellect that can be part of falling in love."

In the last twenty years, we have become accustomed to seeing women make new beginnings when their children leave home. It will take a while to realize how often men also make such new beginnings and how many women make them more than once. We are like cats with nine lives, landing once again on our feet. One of the things we have in common is a reluctance to discard the past and a willingness to look back for whatever may still fit, like a line of Arabic poetry pulled up from memory from twenty years before.

Johnnetta and Alice, the two women in the group who have been divorced, have both had important and lasting relationships with their ex-husbands. "Divorce sounds like such a total affair," Johnnetta said, "but really you're only ending certain parts of certain relationships. Robert is not divorced from his sons and Robert and I are not divorced in a total sense. So you continue to work out all the other parts of the relationships. You continue some and you re-create others. When we divorced, Robert's work was disrupted by the upheavals in Grenada, so when we came to the final arrangements, my lawyer said they were an embarrassment. 'Lady, you're gonna run me out of the profession!' "

No wonder the lawyer was upset. For Johnnetta approached the settlement with the conviction that what was most important was to make sure their sons could visit either parent and find them in a situation of some dignity. This was more important to her than who got what money and how much.

My mother used to boast that she maintained friendships with each of her three ex-husbands and, most of the time, with their wives. The discontinuities associated with divorce and remarriage are becoming more and more common, partly because there is more time for growth and change in a lengthened life span. Gradually, we are learning to include them within the framework of a life, to say of a marriage that has ended that it was good while it lasted. "I have this theory," Alice said, "that if one has nontrivial relationships, it isn't wholesome just to write them off, it leaves a hard sort of thing. So if one can just transform them into something else . . . I think friendship is a possible sort of thing. I don't think it's ever possible to lose a long-term relationship. You can't remove it from your brain, so you have to deal with what remains. Paul is an important part of my life even though we're divorced. We were married for thirteen years. So the best thing is to transform the relationship, not to assume it's dead. There are a lot of opportunities people have to transform things, but one has to work at them, and it's not always easy. Like becoming a virtuoso, you have to practice a lot, and the same thing with feelings. And it's not logical."

It was interesting that Jack's wife, Jean, tried to maintain positive relations with Alice for some time, even after Jack's death, but they didn't hold up once the lawyers were in the picture. "Terrible things happened. Jean's side was very uncool," Alice said, describing the last-minute changes in the terms of the settlement. It seemed clear that the suit had become a matter of personal hostility rather than straight business law. "So I say to the lawyers, 'look, guys, forget it, who gives a rosy?' Anyhow, December 16, 1985, everything is settled. Raw nerve endings notwithstanding, we're into a new stage and negotiations on the representation of the estate on the company board were resolved. I have never felt so much hatred, and that really disturbed me. The thing I feel is most important is to keep one's head straight, and one of the things that does a job on you is negative emotion like hatred. It's taking a long time to dissipate. It's one of those issues that probably will never get resolved. I understand that most people fall prey to negative behavior because they've never practiced. When things are hard you don't necessarily rise to the occasion. But you have to start somewhere. And if one learns from an experience, one is careful in other situations from the beginning."

At one time I would have interpreted Alice's story in religious terms, in terms of the necessity for forgiveness. At another stage in my development, I would have been concerned to affirm that anger too has its place and that it is not healthy to bury it. Today, I am more concerned with the issue of putting the painful and the joyful parts of a life together and convinced that resignation is not the only positive way to do so. Most of the women I worked with on this project share affirmations of unity, of natural beauty, of human interdependence, affirmations that the wholes to be guarded and the goals to be striven for cannot be specified in a fine positivistic mesh or accounted for as dollars and cents, but may be trapped in the vaguer mesh of poetry, like the moon in the boughs of a tree. When the only achievements permitted are those of humility and poverty, you turn them around, echoing the Sermon on the Mount, and say that somehow, somewhere these pains of the present are worth something. But when achievement and satisfaction are a part of the whole, pain can be included also, even in the present.

The word "wisdom" has been part of the Eriksonian formulation of the life cycle from the very beginning, but as Joan and Erik grow older, they have become increasingly interested in the last stage of the life cycle, whose distinctive strength they called wisdom. When Joan sat down to consider the epigenesis of wisdom in relation to artistic creativity—its gradual emergence at every stage of the life cycle—she found herself pursuing the way the term has been used in other times and places and she was struck by how often wisdom had been associated with the feminine.

"It's been very illuminating, because as I read these things, I could see how the scribes of the world have all been men and they've played down what didn't please them or they thought was unimportant and just ignored the feminine elements that were there all the time. It's just nice to take the old form and say look how this is. I was rereading Proverbs to see how close it is to what I was writing, when it talks about Wisdom, or *hokhmah* in Hebrew. And the English keeps saying "she," but there's no mention that Wisdom is a woman. And she's rough, she just tells 'em off, she says, 'Ye sons of men, come to your senses, learn perception!' " Joan went on to talk about other female personifications of wisdom like Sophia or Athena, and the Shaktis that combine themes of vitality and wisdom and compassion in the Far Eastern traditions. "They're the ones the people reach out to. Buddha's not going to help them, he's going to go and sit in a cave and contemplate, but they're too hungry for that, so they reach out to their goddesses. I think it's so touching.

"I talked yesterday at our seminar about the attributes of wisdom, and they're survival skills, and the women have had them all along. I'm not trying to say it in a bellicose way. I've never been a fighting feminist. But if we don't get into the councils of the mighty, we'll go on having wars. We've got to get the sense of what women stand for represented in the top echelons, because they're gonna kill us all. They just don't have what it takes to make for interdependence and interrelationship.

"I went to the American Academy of Arts and Sciences last night and they had a speaker talking on China, and I watched all these characters going around like cocks in their best shirts, and their wives, many of them, just pulling out of the fray. And I looked at one of them and winked and I said, 'How about that? I like the edges too, there's not enough room in the middle there.' It was such a funny evening. I just chuckle to myself."

There is a curious leap here, from the female deities and archetypes to the problems of actual women, from shrines and temples to the edges of a room filled with prestigious scholars, those margins where new visions may be born. Usually we think of wisdom in terms of loftly abstractions, not survival skills, absolute truths, not tactful equivocations. No one expects Athena to be streetwise; even less do we expect that virgin goddess to be what you might call hearthwise, to embody a homespun wisdom of relationships and sensory richness. And yet the central survival skill is surely the capacity to pay attention and respond to changing circumstances, to learn and adapt, to fit into new environments beyond the safety of the temple precincts.

ENRICHING
THE EARTH

WOMEN TODAY, trying to compose lives that will honor all their commitments and still express all their potentials with a certain unitary grace, do not have an easy task. It is important, however, to see that, in finding a personal path among the discontinuities and moral ambiguities they face, they are performing a creative synthesis with a value that goes beyond the merely personal. We feel lonely sometimes because each composition is unique, but gradually we are becoming aware of the balances and harmonies that must inform all such compositions. Individual improvisations can sometimes be shared as models of possibility for men and women in the future.

During the seventies, many women believed that if

women were simply admitted to full participation in decision making, the world would be a better place. This no longer seems as simple as it once did. We can see now that those women who succeed in adopting traditional male models leave the world very much as it is, and so we celebrate the success of women who participate on male terms with a certain ambivalence. We no longer see femaleness as guaranteeing a higher degree of caring; rather, we are concerned with the question of how the necessary combinations of caring will be made and how the old divisions of labor, constructed in terms of separate spheres of activity, will be redistributed across genders.

There has been a tendency to look ahead to some sort of utopia in which women will no longer be torn by the conflicting claims and desires that so often turn their pathways into zigzags or, at best, spirals. And yet these very conflicting claims are affirmations of value. It would be easier to live with a greater clarity of ambition, to follow goals that beckon toward a single upward progression. But perhaps what women have to offer in the world today, in which men and women both must learn to deal with new orders of complexity and rapid change, lies in the very rejection of forced choices: work or home, strength or vulnerability, caring or competition, trust or questioning. Truth may not be so simple. The stories in this book are the stories of women who have struggled and improvised to combine different values, paying the price of criticism or rejection by those who expected them to conform to other and older visions. Their purity lies in their embrace of multiplicity.

Many years ago, when my father began to write about

ecology, he speculated that conscious purpose might be a fatal characteristic of the human species, leading human beings to pursue narrowly conceived purposes without an understanding of their destructive effects. At that time, I became convinced that the way to address the problem was by learning new and more inclusive forms of attention or mindfulness. Today, more than twenty years later, I see the next step in the concept of response. It is interesting that, in spite of the different emphasis, the word *response* provides the etymology of *responsibility*, whose central place in women's ethical sensitivities Carol Gilligan has so eloquently investigated.*

The women in this book are deeply concerned with effectiveness, far from the old stereotypes of female passivity, and yet their mode of action is responsive rather than purposive: it is based on looking and listening and touching rather than the pursuit of abstractions. If it is true that the unit of survival is the organism plus its environment, a sensitivity to the environment is the highest of survival skills and not a dangerous distraction. We must live in a wider space and a longer stretch of time. In thinking about survival, we must think of sustaining life across generations rather than accepting the short-term purposes of politicians and accountants.

Each of these women has cared for children and shared intimacy with lovers, but instead of investing their whole lives in these relationships, they have learned modes of ef-

---

*Carol Gilligan, *In a Different Voice: Psychological Theory and Women's Development* (Cambridge, MA: Harvard University Press, 1982).

fectiveness that make them caretakers and homemakers beyond their own families, creating environments for growth or learning, healing or moving toward creative fulfillment, seeking authority as a means rather than as an end. For them, caretaking and homemaking are not alternatives to success and productivity in the male professional or business worlds; they are styles of action in that world based on the recognition that ideas and organizations and imaginative visions also require fostering. Five years ago, Ellen was sharply aware of conflicts between these different roles and saw motherhood as a radical interruption of her professional life; now, with family life reshaped around two children and the last intrusive formalities of Sarah's adoption completed, she is constructing a new version of professional life that affirms something all of us have learned—that our productivity depends on the discovery of new forms of flexibility.

All of these women are conservers, holding onto skills and relationships that may be recycled at a later date. After a long period of grieving for Jack, Alice began to see other men, first a lover she had known just before Jack, then a man of whom she had spoken nostalgically from her years in graduate school. When I finish this manuscript, my next research project will be in Israel, where I will try to revive my knowledge of Hebrew and Arabic, barely used for decades, and pick up old friendships. I will try to understand why some visions are sustained while others fade, much as my mother did when she returned after twenty-five years to re-study a village in New Guinea. Johnnetta, back in the South where she grew up, riding a wave of triumph at Spelman that will affect all the traditionally black colleges, announced her engagement to a man who was a playmate when she was eight years old. Art hopes to work in Atlanta and to explore what it will mean to be the first "first man" of Spelman, to find a model for a new kind of partnership. Joan and Erik have begun to edit the journal Erik kept as a young *Wandervogel* and artist, roving around Europe before he came to rest in Vienna. Joan has been approached for her notes and drafts on the prewar teaching of dance in Europe, for most of the records there were destroyed.

These are not mere byways of nostalgia, for in each case there are new beginnings and potentials for creativity. The relationships and commitments of these women's lives are not disposable; instead, each is treasured for possible recycling. I started this project with a sharp awareness of discontinuities. In an early draft, I wrote bitterly, "Do not pass GO. Do not collect two hundred dollars," referring to the Monopoly cards dealt during the draining interruptions of women's lives. But because the project extended over several years, I had a chance to see interruptions reshaped into transitions as thread after thread from the past was picked up and woven in. As a result, I look at discontinuity differently. The lesson each of us has drawn from multiple fresh starts is that there is always something in the past to work with. Today, Alice has left her company and its future is uncertain. She is still hesitating between different possibilities in the United States and Japan as a researcher or as an executive. By this time, like each of the rest of us, she has enough experience of new beginnings to be skilled in recycling what she has learned in new contexts, and she has the confidence to move forward slowly, doing enough consulting to main-

tain her flexibility. In moments of doubt, I tell myself I have
survived one revolution that wasted the work of years. One
revolution and a coup.

Our lives are full of surprises, for none of us has followed a specific ambition toward a specific goal. Instead,
we have learned from interruptions and improvised from
the materials that came to hand, reshaping and reinterpret-
ing. As a result, all of us have lived with high levels of ambiguity. Johnnetta was once the most radical of the group,
but today she builds within existing institutions; Ellen, with
her intense concern for the needs of homeless families,
works through corporate structures. Absolute solutions
give way to compromises, but the compromises are organic
hybrids able to flourish in a complex ecosystem that
spreads more widely and endures longer than we would
once have imagined. None of us follows a single vision; instead, our very visions are products of growth and adaptation, not fixed but emergent.

We all work too hard, burning too many candles, driven
by a sense of how much needs to be done. Johnnetta is
hounded by invitations, for the image she can offer is rare
and badly needed. She worries that quality will be compro-
mised under pressure, but this is part of a life whose theme
is response rather than purpose, response that makes us
more broadly attentive, rather than purpose that might narrow our view.

None of us is a superwoman. As we get older we increasingly must worry about conserving energy, avoiding fatigue
and jet lag and stress, caring for our bodies and our minds
instead of spending them carelessly, so there will be more to

give. This is not a matter of having it all, for the hours of the day and the vitality of our bodies are indeed limited. It is a matter of having more, for each of us has discovered, in spite of double-shift labor and competing demands, that we are nurtured by our work and that we can combine different kinds of tasks so they feed each other—mostly—instead of competing.

Implicit in everything we do is a longing for synergy, a hope that when there are competing demands on our time or strength we can find non-zero-sum solutions—not this replacing that, but this enhancing that. For once, the images of patchwork and weaving seem to me inadequate. Instead, I visualize one of those oriental puzzles, with its seemingly arbitrary pieces spread across the tabletop, which may some-how be fitted together to form a perfect sphere. Joan and Erik live now in a house they share with two younger colleagues, where public and private, home and work, effort and play are coiled and fitted together. I constantly try to combine trips, to piggyback one task on another; whenever an invitation comes that will take me to a distant city, I schedule other visits or meetings around it, and travel home exhausted. It's not surprising that I tried at Amherst to persuade departments that copiers or buses or even academic appointments could be shared, for I have spent much of my life stretching resources to respond to multiple needs. At the worst times, when you encounter someone aggressively unwilling to share, you dream of being dismembered, cut up to meet competing demands. Children's tantrums dissolve into sunshine, but the habits of exclusive self-interest are disheartening in highly educated adults. Still, when the combinations work, you can believe you have enriched the earth.

There is a habit of mind that grows from this way of experiencing one's own limits and potentials that may lead toward societal solutions. The fundamental problem of our society and our species today is to discover a way to flourish that will not be at the expense of some other community or of the biosphere, to replace competition with creative interdependence. At present, we are steadily depleting the planet of resources and biological diversity; the developed world thrives on the poverty of the south. We are in need of an understanding of global relationships that will be not only sustainable but also enriching; it must come to us as a positive challenge, a vision worth fulfilling, not a demand for retrenchment and austerity. This is of course what we do day by day when we refuse to accept the idea that we must reject one part of life to enhance another. Projecting a new vision is artistic; it's a task each of us pursues in composing our lives. One can write songs about sharing; it is hard to write songs about limits.

Solutions to problems often depend on how they are defined. If you look at unfolding lives, you immediately become aware of the processes of redefinition: shelters may come to be seen as constraining walls, interruptions are recognized as moments of fertilization, outrage becomes empowering and freeing. It is possible to look for pattern in seeming disorder and to propose a search for potential benefit in every problem. The strategies we follow are not strategies for victory but for survival and adaptation. Perhaps what we are learning today about the victims of homelessness will provide a clearer vision of the kind of support that every child or adult needs; perhaps celebrating diversity within the African diaspora will answer some of the questions about diversity in American society; perhaps a collection of broken beads can be joined in a necklace of elegance and beauty.

The visions we construct will not be classic pioneer visions of struggle and self-reliance. Rather, they will involve an intricate elaboration of themes of complementarity—forms of mutual completion and enhancement and themes of recognition achieved through loving attention. All the forms of life we encounter—not only colleagues and neighbors, but other species, other cultures, the planet itself—are similar to us and similarly in need of nurture, but there is also a larger whole to which all belong. The health of that larger whole is essential to the health of the parts. Many women raised in male-dominated cultures have to struggle against the impulse to sacrifice their health for the health of the whole, to maintain complementarity without dependency. But many men raised in the same traditions have to struggle against pervasive imageries in which their own health or growth is a victory achieved at the expense of the other. We have perhaps a few years in which to combine these. The visions will be both like and unlike familiar religious visions: like, in that they involve the hesitation of reverence before acting to change, the attentive appreciation of the sacredness of what is; unlike, in that they are open. Instead of worshipping ancestors or deities conceived as parents, we must celebrate the mysterious sacredness of that which is still to be born.

Meantime, the five women of this book continue in the

microcosms of their lives, shaping our own lyric commentaries on the world around us. Each of us constructs a life that is her own central metaphor for thinking about the world. But of course these lives do not look like parables or allegories. Mostly, they look like ongoing improvisations, quite ordinary sequences of day-to-day events. They continue to unfold. Even as this book ends, the visions are still emerging, the five artists are still at work, as e.e. cummings says, ". . . placing carefully there a strange thing and a known thing here . . . and without breaking anything." The compositions we create in these times of change are filled with interlocking messages of our commitments and decisions. Each one is a message of possibility.